'This compelling, comprehensive apt-titled b[...] leaders at any level. Numerous real-life examples and quotable quotes are seamlessly woven with masterful elaborate text in a sequential manner from the start to finish. There is enough arsenal in this book to help you master your own destiny and assist others in doing the same.'

Kosam Nyamdela
MoP, PMP, MBusAn, MBA Strategic Planning

'*First, Lead Yourself* by Cillín Hearns certainly isn't the stereotypical paint by numbers approach to coaching books. Instead it is full insightful stories of someone I have got to know but didn't know. A book about how to become extraordinary for the average person. Open, Read, Think.'

Nick Roberts
CEO, Momentum Consulting Group

'Our team has been fortunate to experience transformational work with Cillín. Now, with *First, Lead Yourself*, his self-led development approach mixing stories and exercises is available to everyone.'

Stevo O'Rourke
Director, Ocular

'This book is amazing, I had so many 'aha' moments. Although not really a self-help book, I've learnt so much about myself from Cillín, I'm now more comfortable being me and more aware of my personal rules, I didn't realise I had so many! The wisdom Cillín shares has enabled me to become more resilient, a better leader, and most importantly, a better parent. '

Luke Johnston
Director, Double-O Consulting

'I have had the pleasure of working with Cillín Hearns in my professional career and I was very excited to read this book. This is an inspirational and helpful book indeed! His approach is very practical and there is something for everyone to take away from this book whether you are dealing with work, colleagues, kids or many other aspects of your personal life. I enjoyed how Cillín was able to relate his personal journey into the books narrative; it showcased his honest and pragmatic approach to life and used real life scenarios to demonstrate methods and ways to improve one's self. This isn't a book you would read only once – this is a book that you will hang on to and pull out time and time again. I highly recommend to friends and colleagues alike.'

Mariska Carlson-Smith
General Manager, Velocity


'Too often books about leadership jump right in at the high level. Generally the author is a success in his particular sphere of influence and as such anticipates his readership will also be operating at a similar level. Seldom is there a book about leadership that recognises the single most important factor; leadership of self. In *First, Lead Yourself*, Cillín draws from years of experience in the corporate world where his leadership and coaching has assisted many in getting started on their leadership path. His book is a reflection of that graft and journey. Written with unapologetic vulnerability and full of useful, tangible tactics that we can all use to improve or begin our leadership experience, this book is so much more than just a leadership "instruction manual".'

Stew Darling
founder of the Lead through Life Programme
and stewdarling.com

# First, Lead Yourself

# First, Lead Yourself

*Practical Tools to Unleash Your*
*Leadership Potential*

## Cillín Hearns

RESULTS COACHING

The web addresses referenced in this book were live and correct at the time of the book's publication but may be subject to change.

Hearns, Cillín
    First, lead yourself : Practical tools to unleash your leadership potential / Cillín Hearns.
     Pages cm
    Includes bibliographical references.
    ISBN 978-0-47346-191-1

Illustrations by Kim Quirke.

*To my beautiful wife, Louise,*

*and my amazing daughters, Sophie and Ciara.*

*You have taught me what love really means.*

# Contents

Contents

## Part Two: Bouncing Back

## Part Three: Artful Communication

# Foreword

Everyone should be their own CEO.

Today, whether we like it or not, we live in a world where anything can be operated like a business or everyone is like an independent company. The only difference is—all the commercial companies are *limited liability*, but our own *company* is *unlimited*. We need to use our time, reputation, credit, and everything else we can to assure success.

We need to lead ourselves like we would lead a business: understand our core strengths and weaknesses, build collaboration with others, create our own products and services, maintain our personal reputation, focus on better cost and benefit, etc. All the concepts, exercises and methods in this book come from Cillín's professional practice and have been proven many times in the real world.

In the past, we used these skills to lead a real business.

Now, you can apply them to lead yourself.

I am delighted to have had the opportunity to read the early draft of this book. To the best of my knowledge, most of the contents only appear in the in-house coaching and training Cillín delivers to his corporate clients. Now, he is your *private coach* and has presented all that knowledge, hands-on suggestions, and strategies ready for you to absorb in *First, Lead Yourself.*

Let us assume your *Unlimited Company* has just been established and, as the CEO, please lead yourself and enjoy the journey.

Dr. Richard Li

14th November 2018

## Note to the Reader

There are a couple of things I'd like to share with you before we get started. Firstly, throughout time, stories have been used to share meaning and understanding. Several stories are dotted between the chapters, and each of them is directly related to the content. Some are short and some are a little longer, but I hope you find all of them are enjoyable.

Secondly, grab a notebook and a pen and keep them on hand as you work your way through each of the exercises. As your knowledge of yourself deepens, you may find yourself going back over what you thought was relevant at that time, but may need to be tweaked the further you progress. The only way to do this properly is to write everything down and keep it in the same place.

As a final point, be honest and realistic with yourself as you work your way through the pages. I hope the lessons in these pages change your life the way they have mine and hundreds of my clients.

Enjoy the journey!

# What You Must Understand First

*As you grow as a leader, the attention from the self must expand to include awareness of others and their needs.*

Every leadership book you ever read is likely to reference self-awareness, but awareness alone is not enough. Although it's where we start—in fact, it's the only place we can start!—you must also be aware of others and your organisation and environment.

Allow me to introduce you to the Awareness Triangle, an essential tool for leaders at every stage of development.

What impact do you have on others, and how do they impact you throughout your day? What impact are you having on your environment, and what impact is it having on you?

Lastly, as a leader, it's important to recognise the impact others are having on their environment and, of course, the impact the environment is having on them. If the impact is negative in any of the above instances, we need to make a change.

**The Awareness Triangle**

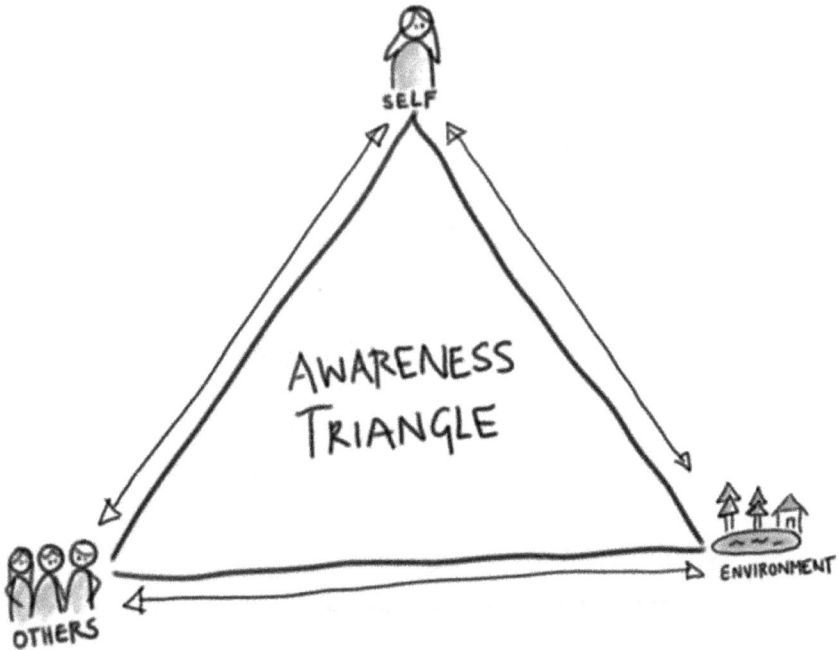

## The Self and Others

The more we become aware of ourselves and start to understand why we do the things we do, the more we start to understand others and why they do the things they do. When we follow the left side of the triangle between Self and Others, we recognise there must be certain skills we need to work on for us to get the best out of the relationship. These skills include the following:

- Communication
- Collaboration

- Conflict Management
- Personal Working Styles
- Motivation
- Negotiation

## *The Self and the Organisation/Environment*

Looking at the opposite side of the Awareness Triangle, which links Self and Environment, we recognise that the environment can also impact who we are and how we behave. In order to perform at your very best, there are certain things you need to have in place:

- Your personal vision
- A vision for the organisation/team
- Your personal goals
- A strategy (and clear objectives) for the organisation/team
- Measures of success
- A clear set of values for the organisation/team

## *Others and the Organisation/Environment*

As you grow as a leader, the attention from the self must expand to include awareness of others and their needs. We must start paying attention to the impact others are having on the environment and vice versa, especially when the organisation is going through change or major challenges. As a leader, some of the skills needed to support and grow your team are as follows:

- Facilitation
- Leadership styles and when to use them
- Situational leadership
- Applying the team lifecycle and how this impacts people

- Understanding the change lifecycle and how this impacts people

This book shines a spotlight on the first steps of leadership that we all must take if we are going to be the type of leaders that people follow. There is a difference, of course. You can be a leader by default, such as because of your title. I call that leading through authority, and it is a particularly weak form of leadership. Then there is true leadership, where people follow you regardless of title. People follow you because of who you are.

I wish you every success on your journey. As with any personal change, it doesn't come without work. But if there is one piece of advice I can give you before you begin, it is to put into practice everything you learn.

And remember, contrary to popular wisdom, "knowledge is not power—it's potential power." ~ Anthony Robbins

# PART ONE

# Know Thyself

*Self-awareness is our capacity to stand apart from ourselves and examine our thinking, our motives, our history, our scripts, our actions, and our habits and tendencies.*

~ Stephen Covey

# The Monk and the Student

*I*t was a beautiful morning for the journey, and the two monks made their way down the hillside into the valley on their way to a neighbouring monastery. It was a full day's walk, and the men settled into a comfortable stride, the older monk easily keeping pace with the younger. After some time, and not wasting the opportunity to spend time with one of the senior members of the monastery, the younger monk asked a question that was on his mind.

*"Master, why is man so troubled?"*

*The older monk thought for a time before answering his young disciple by way of a story.*

*There was once a time when all human beings were gods, but they so abused their divinity that Brahma, the chief god, decided to take it away from them and hide it where it would never be found. But where to hide their divinity was the question.*

*So Brahma called a council of the gods to help him decide.*

*"Let's bury it deep in the earth," said the gods.*

*But Brahma answered, "No, that will not do, because humans will dig into the earth and find it."*

*Then the gods said, "Let's sink it into the deepest ocean."*

*But Brahma said, "No, not there, for they will learn to dive into the ocean and will find it."*

*Then the gods said, "Let's take it to the top of the highest mountain and hide it there."*

*But once again Brahma replied, "No, that will not do either, because they will eventually climb every mountain and once again take up their divinity."*

*Then the gods gave up and said, "We do not know where to hide it, because it seems that there is no place on earth or in the sea that human beings will not eventually reach."*

*Brahma thought for a long time, and then said, "This is what we will do. We will hide their divinity deep in the centre of their own being, for humans will never think to look for it there."*

*All the gods agreed that this was the perfect hiding place, and the deed was done.*

*And since that time, humans have been searching the earth, digging, diving, climbing, and exploring—seeking something already deep within themselves.*

# CHAPTER 1

# Who Am I Really?

*This sense of, 'I'm not enough,' is the seed that leads to the creation of the False Self.*

W ind the clock back several years, and you would have found me in a boardroom giving a presentation on the direction of project management to a group of general managers. Two minutes into my talk, the Chief Financial Officer interjects with the question, "Who has given you the mandate to this?"

I had been warned ahead of time that he might do this. He was clearly challenging my authority, and it triggered something within me. There was no way I was going to have my role questioned like this. I had no choice but to defend myself, and I wasn't backing down.

We ended up exchanging words as the rest of the people in the room watched and tried to interject gently. I blatantly pushed on with my weakening resolve, until I heard the distinctive sound in the distance… the death knell of my future with that organisation.

I left the meeting shaking with anger, more at myself than at anything else. This wasn't the first time I'd lost my temper when I felt I was being forced into a corner. I was frustrated and angry at myself. Why did I act this way? I could put it down to being red-headed and Irish, but deep inside, I knew there were some demons I had to face.

## Meet Your Self

To understand the self, we need to go back to our formative years, between the ages of zero and seven. It's during this time in our lives that the foundations of our personality are formed. When a child is born, he or she is driven by a single evolutionary code—survival. For example, the nervous system has inbuilt responses, such as rooting, which causes the child to turn its head, open its mouth, and start sucking when the cheek or mouth is stroked; another inbuilt response is grasping, which is triggered by touching the infant's palms.

These physical responses dissipate during the first few months of a child's life, but a deeper aspect of our survival is more enduring. This is our enduring need for love and acceptance born out of a child's absolute dependence on others for survival.

Therefore, during our formative years, our core internal focus is on developing strategies to gain love from those who can guarantee our survival. To achieve this, we take on their values, their beliefs and their rules. Our actions are driven by the need to gain their acceptance—to gain their love. We learn that to be loved, we need to meet certain standards, and so we distort ourselves into being what significant others in our life want. We develop what Carl Rogers calls 'conditions of worth'.

Of course, during these years we don't have the cognitive ability to question these values or beliefs, and we accept them without much thought. As we grow older, we've been wearing this 'psychological' mask for so long, we think it's who we are. However, who we have been projecting to the world is not our true self, but who we've been shaped to become by our desire for love and acceptance.

Psychologists refer to these different selves as the *True Self* and the *False Self.* A stereotypical example might be the accountant who has a passion for music and creativity, but followed her parents' advice about getting a 'real job'. Every day she goes to work miserable and pines to break free.

When the gap between the True Self and the False Self becomes too great, it can trigger a range of unhealthy emotions and lead to uncertainty, anxiety, and depression. To avoid these painful emotions, we may distort our behaviour or the way we see ourselves. In other words, to meet people's internalised expectations of us, we abandon our talents and inclinations, ignoring our own needs and feelings. Commonly referred to as Imposter Syndrome, there is an unhealthy stress associated with living a life that we believe to be false.

Figure 1-1 represents a rather proud looking individual in the centre of an eclipse that signifies the False Self. The False Self can manifest itself in several ways, and although we're never just one 'type', we do tend to gravitate to a preferred way of being, especially under times of stress.

But before we examine the individual types, let's examine how the False Self is formed.

## The Birth of the Self

When a mother who is bio-chemically normal gives birth, her system is flooded with a hormone called oxytocin. In fact, it is oxytocin that induces the birthing process. Known as the cuddle hormone, it causes us to feel good when we're around other people we like. When we get a hug from someone, our brain emits oxytocin and we have positive, bonding feelings. (Unless we get a hug from a person we don't like, and well, that's just creepy.)

If you've ever had the experience of being part of a great team—you're all working hard, you're sharing a laugh, the energy is high, and there are high fives going around—it's likely your body was producing oxytocin, which is helping you form a bond with your teammates.

Now, if you get this feel-good feeling toward another person just from a hug, imagine what a mother feels when her system is flooded with this hormone! She can't help but love this child... even if it looks like a monkey, it's the most beautiful and precious thing in the world. There is nothing the child can do wrong! When the mother is regaling the latest incident to her friends, she may start off with, "You'll never guess what that little scamp did this morning," with a big grin on her face and feeling nothing but love.

So the child is bathed in a sea of unconditional love. But that doesn't last forever, does it? Things tend to change a little when she gets a little more ambulatory and starts reaching for things that may cause her harm. She spies a plug socket and reckons her little fingers

FIGURE 1-1

**The False Self**

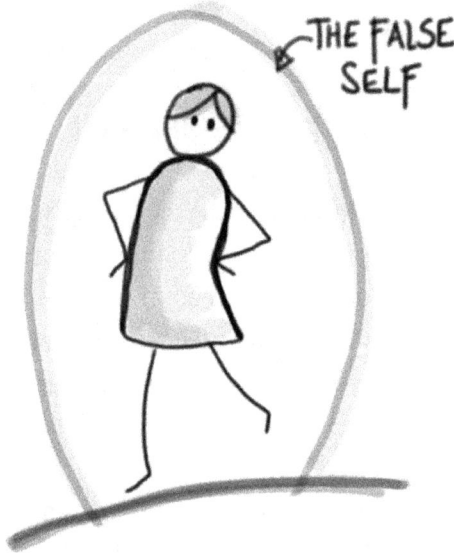

would fit nicely in there. In fact, if I were to ask you the first word a child understands (not the first word a child learns to say), I imagine you'd guess it straight away: 'No!'

So here I am feeling loved, feeling free to explore my environment knowing I can do nothing wrong, when all of a sudden, I hear 'No!' And the person I hear this from is the most important person in my life—my lifeline, the person I rely most on in this world for survival. I begin to realise that maybe there are conditions to receiving love after all. As a child, all I want to do is to get back to that unconditional love, to be accepted... because my survival depends on it.

Anthony Robbins sums this up nicely when he states that our greatest fear is "that I am not enough, and if I'm not enough, I won't be loved." That feeling of being not enough can be different from one person to the next.

---

*Insert yours here:* I'm not _____enough.

*At this point I want to tell you this belief is rubbish, and if it is holding you back in any way, then read on, because we're going to shatter that belief for you in the next couple of chapters.*

---

This sense of 'I'm not enough' is the seed that leads to the creation of the False Self. Let me give you an example.
I'm two or three years old and I'm playing with my blocks. I place them one on top of the other until I make a rudimentary tower. My mother walks in and says, "Cillín, did you build that all by yourself?" Her tone is full of praise as she picks me up and gives me kisses and hugs. I'm feeling pretty good about this exchange, because I'm getting all that love and attention every child craves.

FIGURE 1-2

**I'm Not Enough**

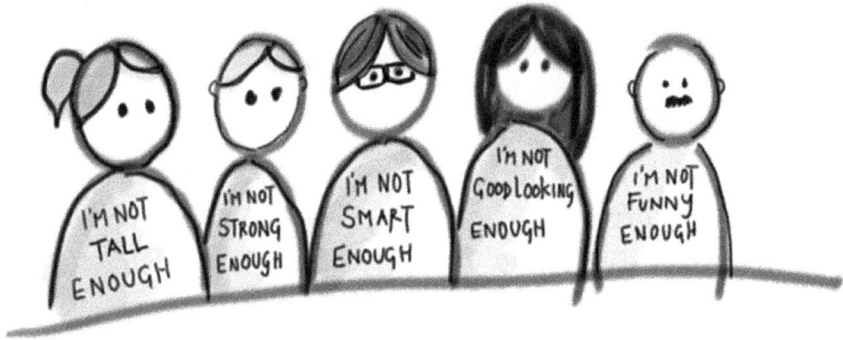

A few days later, my father walks in while I'm driving my self-made Lego car. He too picks me up and praises me for making something. It doesn't take long before I link up that when I do things—when I *achieve* things—I get positive attention. I get a lot of love.

Very soon, an Achiever is born!

Or, what about the scenario when uncle Colin comes around for dinner. I'm in my highchair, a little bored, with my mashed potatoes, so I flick a piece and it lands on uncle Colin's face. Everyone laughs uproariously, and I get loads of attention for doing something funny. Again, the next time I do something that makes people laugh, I get loads of attention.

Very soon, a Comedian is born!

Figure 1-3 illustrates the many ways our false self can manifest itself. However, it's important to note that though we're made up of several 'personas,' we tend to gravitate toward a dominant one, especially during times of stress.

FIGURE 1-3

**The Many Personas of the False Self**

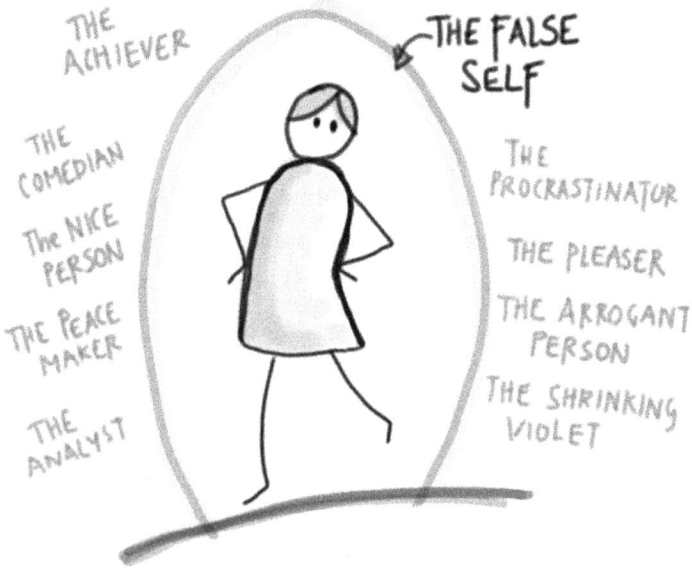

THE ACHIEVER
THE COMEDIAN
The NICE PERSON
THE PEACE MAKER
THE ANALYST
THE FALSE SELF
THE PROCRASTINATOR
THE PLEASER
THE ARROGANT PERSON
THE SHRINKING VIOLET

This is because the unconscious mind, although extremely powerful and capable of amazing things, is inherently lazy. If it has a strategy that has worked in the past, it will continue to go there again and again until we develop a new strategy and replace the old one.

When we're under attack, perceived or real, the unconscious mind doesn't tend to think too far into the future; its primary function is about our survival in the moment. So if we're under pressure, like in a boardroom being challenged, our brain goes into fight or flight mode and calls on strategies that have worked in the past. Unfortunately, however, what may have worked for us in the playground might not work for us now as adults.

"But coach," I hear you ask, "being an Achiever is a good thing, isn't it? Getting things done is a good thing."

I agree… to a point. All of these personas are useful in their context. Let's imagine them on a continuum (Figure 1-4). As you can see, personas at the extremes can have detrimental impacts. So what we're looking for is the sweet spot between these extremes.

We develop these personas because we are conditioned by significant others in our lives. These personas are nothing more than strategies to gain love and to be accepted, which is vital to our survival.

We often carry these strategies into our adult years, continuously calling on them when we feel under pressure or we doubt ourselves. But as mentioned previously, what worked for us as children may not work for us as adults.

FIGURE 1-4

**Personas on a Continuum**

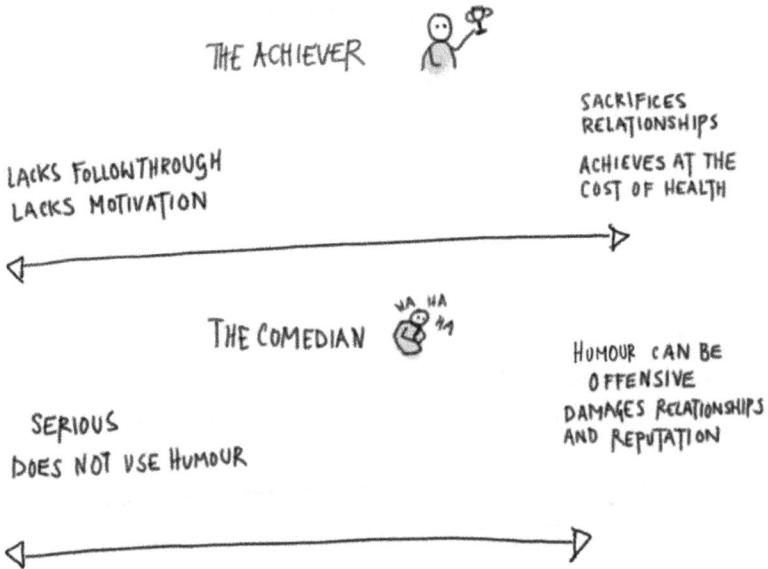

THE ACHIEVER

SACRIFICES
RELATIONSHIPS

ACHIEVES AT THE
COST OF HEALTH

LACKS FOLLOWTHROUGH
LACKS MOTIVATION

THE COMEDIAN

HUMOUR CAN BE
OFFENSIVE
DAMAGES RELATIONSHIPS
AND REPUTATION

SERIOUS
DOES NOT USE HUMOUR

## Other Aspects of the Self

Before we explore how to change these old and potentially harmful strategies, let's consider other aspects of the self and how they can lead to unhelpful emotions. Figure 1-5 illustrates the relationship between the Actual Self, the Ought Self, and the Ideal Self.

The Actual Self is our view of who we are; the Ideal Self is the self that we strive to become and represents our aspirations (a future version of ourselves); and the Ought Self includes the obligations and responsibilities that define the way we ought to be (this view represents the expectations others have of us, or the expectations that we have of ourselves, which sometimes can be unhealthy and unrealistic). We have different Actual, Ideal, and Ought Selves from a number of points of view, including our own and those of significant others in our life.

FIGURE 1-5

**The Ought Self and the Ideal Self**

A perceived discrepancy between our Actual Self and our Ideal Self can lead to painful emotions of disappointment, dissatisfaction, shame, and embarrassment. Similarly, a perceived gap between our Actual Self and our Ought Self can lead to anxiety, fear, resentment, and guilt. Research into the discrepancy between these selves indicates that they influence not only our mood but also our physical health.

## Tapping into Your True Self

As I mentioned earlier, when the gap between the True Self and the False Self becomes too great, it can cause harmful and often uncomfortable emotions. Therefore, our goal is to reduce this gap so we can tap into who we truly are. When we do this, all the fears, doubts, and uncertainties about ourselves fall away. We develop a core sense of being untainted by the demands of others.

To reduce this gap, we need to understand a little about how the brain works. Imagine a person walking through a field overgrown with grass. Initially, they create a thin trail of flattened grass. However, if more and more traffic follows the same path, the track becomes wider, until eventually it becomes a superhighway and traffic can travel down the path at high speeds.

This is analogous to how our brain processes thoughts. Whenever we have a thought, our brain creates a neuro-association (a connection between two brain cells). The more often we have this thought, the stronger this connection becomes, and the faster the message is transferred between neurons. So fast, in fact, that sometimes we might be feeling upset or angry and we can't figure out why! One downside of negative thoughts is that they tend to have 'babies' (Figure 1-6).

Rarely do we stop with a single negative thought; instead, we get on a roll and we catastrophise. Some people are really good at this, and they spiral ever further downward, consumed by negative thought patterns and becoming completely blind to other possibilities.

FIGURE 1-6

---

**The Brain and Neuro-Associations**

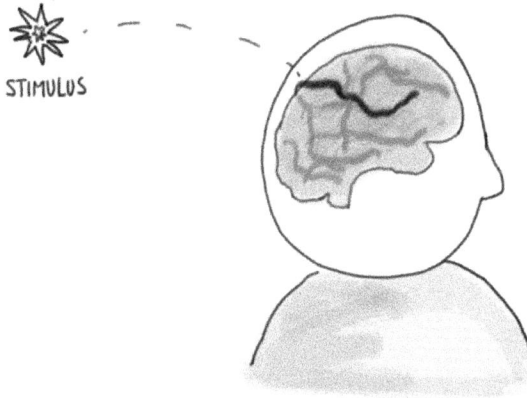

STIMULUS

---

Therefore, to make changes, we must change our thought patterns. Changing how we think about ourselves (self-concept) has a direct impact on how we feel about ourselves (self-esteem), which has a direct impact on our belief about our ability to succeed in specific situations or accomplish a task (self-efficacy). Our self-efficacy has a major impact on how we approach goals, tasks, and challenging situations.

The following exercise is one that I have used with several of my clients over the years, and the effects can be quite profound. It often changes how they perceive situations. As one client expressed, "Even though the triggers that used to cause me to react are still the same, I find that I respond differently, I'm more in control... more confident."

## Developing Your Coat of Arms

The following exercise will take you through a series of steps to develop what I fondly call a Coat of Arms. It represents who you are as a person, what you stand for, and what's important to you; it brings you closer to who you truly are at your core.

Its second purpose is to ward off the slings and arrows of your mind and instil within you the confidence to move forward, even through your toughest times.

As a working example of a coat of arms, I will provide a case study of Eric as you move through the individual steps. You may find it useful to refer to this case study as you work through each step.

### Case Study: Eric's Coat of Arms

Eric is very successful in his career, but suffered from Imposter Syndrome. He lacked confidence and would consistently doubt his abilities, especially in business meetings. He wished he could be more assertive and more articulate when delivering a message. Eric also wished he could be calmer and more measured, be less reactive to hot-button questions, and demonstrate more gravitas as a leader.

### Step 1: Identify your most inspirational moments

Find somewhere quiet for about an hour, somewhere you won't be disturbed. Now, think back to the times in your life when you felt moments of inspiration. When I say inspiration, I don't necessarily mean motivation. The moment could be as subtle as looking at a piece of artwork and being completely drawn to it; it has a deeper meaning to you than it might have for others (I've got one on my desk as I write these words!). It could be a moment of great achievement, one that challenged you to your very core. One where you had to overcome those nagging doubts and fears, but you kept going, you persisted, and you came out on the other side with a new belief about yourself and what's possible. It could be an emotional moment that touched you deeply and changed you in some way.

Another way of identifying inspirational moments is to examine turning points in your life and draw a line from then to now. How did you overcome a tough time? What did you do, and how have you changed since that time?

Take a moment to write these down in your notebook now.

---

**Step 1: Eric's Top Three Inspirational Moments**

1. Speaking at his graduation ceremony

2. Rescuing a failing programme of work that was vital to the success of the organisation

3. Overcoming his fear of diving

---

### Step 2: Choose your top three

Now that you have your list, choose your top three moments. Write a description of each moment as if you're telling a story to another person, focusing on the question, "What is it about this moment that is inspirational for you?"

You may think it's so obvious to you that you don't need to write it down, but don't shortcut the process; every step is important. Fully articulate why this moment is inspirational to you.

Ideally, we're after about a half-page to a full page for each moment. When you've completed the first one, move onto the next. The trick is to just start writing and keep going.

### Step 3: Summarise the key content

For this next step, I want you to imagine that you are a coach. Your client has just shared with you their most inspirational moments. As you review them, underline or summarise the key phrases and moments that you think your client needs to take away with them after your coaching session.

**Step 2: Eric Speaking at His Graduation Ceremony**

Eric was asked to be the speaker at his IT degree graduation ceremony. He was asked to speak at the event because the person who was scheduled to speak pulled out at the last moment. He remembers looking out at a sea of people and nervously walking across the stage to the podium in complete silence. To add to his nervousness, there were Members of Parliament and senior business people in the audience. His parents had flown over especially for the event, and they were very proud. As nervous as he was, he went up onto the stage and nailed it! The crowd laughed in all the right places, and the applause was fantastic. Eric remembers getting all the comments from the crowd about how funny he was and how much they enjoyed his speech. All of that was inspirational to Eric, because it was about just going up and having to do it. He had never spoken publicly before, and now he was speaking in front of a thousand people. It was a huge sense of *WOW! I just did that*!

At the end of this exercise, you will have a set of key phrases that make you who you are. They may be moments that remind you of what you're capable of when the chips are down, or about what's most important to you in life.

**Step 3: Graduation Ceremony - Summarising the Content**
- I just jumped in and did it
- Had everyone in hysterics
- Felt a huge sense of pride
- Put myself out there

**Step 4: Identify the nouns that describe your best qualities**

Now, using your summary as a guide, write the nouns that describe you. To check if the word is a noun, prefix it with "I am a ..." or "I am an ..." If the word doesn't fit, then it's not a noun. Ideally, we're looking for single-word nouns that are positive descriptors of you. Don't try to organize them yet, either. Just write the words all over the page in random places.

If there's a word or a phrase that describes you, but you can't turn it into a noun, jot it down anyway. Once you're done, double-check to ensure you've captured all the words that describe you as a person.

For those words or phrases that are difficult to translate into nouns, think of a symbol or metaphor to capture the meaning.

Table 1-1

**Translating Nouns into Symbols or Metaphors**

| Word/Phrase | Noun |
|---|---|
| Nothing is impossible | Pioneer |
| Faith | Believer |
| Determined | Lion |
| See things through | Finisher |
| Stand up for self | Warrior |
| Mental toughness | Rock |
| Intelligent | Owl |
| Things get easier | Optimist |
| Toughness | Diamond |
| Overcoming obstacles | Mountaineer |
| Patient | Monk |
| Growth | Oak |

Table 1-1 above provides a few examples from some of my clients of the phrases that describe them and the corresponding nouns that sum up the meaning of each phrase; for example, if a person has the belief that *nothing is impossible,* they might capture the meaning of that phrase in the noun *pioneer.* The words don't need to be in the dictionary; what's important to capture is the meaning behind them.

---

**Step 4: Nouns (Personas) Created from Eric's Summary Notes**

Thriver

Overcomer

Conqueror      Winner

Speaker

~~Diver~~      Adapter

Viking

Experiencer

Performer      Creator

~~Doer~~

Influencer      ~~Impossible is nothing~~      Guru

Achiever      ~~Adventurer~~

Comedian

Pioneer

Leader

---

As you can see from Eric's example, some words were swapped for others; for example, 'Impossible is nothing' was replaced with

'Adventurer' and then again with 'Pioneer'. Make sure the right meaning is captured for you.

## Step 5: Highlight key nouns

Now select three random words (try not to select words that are next to or close to one another). Repeat these words to yourself and ask, "Which of these means more to me than the others?" Don't think about this too long; trust your unconscious mind. Put a tick (✓) next to the word that comes out on top and a cross (✗) next to the other two. Repeat this process, choosing words at random. When a word has two crosses (✗✗) next to it, put a line through it. This word is eliminated from the list. When you have four to five words remaining,

---

**Step 5: Prioritisation of Eric's Personas**     ✗✗
~~Overcomer~~

✓✓✓
**Thriver**

✓✗✗          ✓✗✗
~~Conqueror~~   ~~Winner~~

✗✗
~~Speaker~~

✗✗

~~Diver~~ ✓✓✗      ~~Adapter~~
**Viking**

✓✗✗          ~~Experiencer~~
~~Performer~~   ✗✓✗          ✗✗
~~Creator~~

✗✗          ~~Doer~~ ✗✗
~~Influencer~~   ~~Impossible is~~   ~~Guru~~
~~nothing~~
✓✓✗
**Achiever**   ~~Adventurer~~          ✗✗
~~Comedian~~

✗✗          **Pioneer**
~~Leader~~          ✓✓✓

---

write them down on a separate sheet of paper.

### Step 6: Order these words in terms of importance to you

Review your list and check to ensure that none of your words mean the same thing; for example, if 'Guru' and 'Expert' are on your list and they have the same meaning to you, put a line through the least dominant one.

Now, prioritise the remaining words in terms of importance to you. Select the top three. These are your three personas.

---

**Step 6: Ordering Eric's Personas**

| | | |
|---|---|---|
| Thriver | - | 2 |
| Viking | - | 1 |
| Achiever | - | 3 |
| Pioneer | - | 4 |

---

### Step 7: Expand on the meaning

Write your highest priority persona at the top of a separate piece of paper. Create three columns down the page and write 'Me', 'Others', and 'Environment' at the top of each column.

---

**Step 7: Expanding the Meaning for Eric's Viking Persona**

| Me | Others | Environment |
|---|---|---|
| • Confidence | • Pace is deliberate | • Things get |
| • Leadership | and determined | delivered |
| • Strength of | • Clarity | • Make things |
| conviction | • Assurance | happen |
| • Decisive | • Purpose | • We achieve goals |

Now, answer this question, writing your answer in each column as appropriate: "When you are being a [persona] fully and completely, what are the <u>positive</u> impacts on yourself, others, and the environment?"

*Ego is to the true self what a flashlight is to a spotlight.*
~ John Bradshaw

**Step 8: Write out your coat of arms**
Using the words and phrases from the three columns, create your coat of arms description for that persona.

When you read your description, it should speak to you, resonating deeply within you. If it doesn't resonate with you straight away, think of words that evoke images, sounds and feeling; if you get it on the first go, that's great! If not, keep playing around with it until it speaks to you.

Then do the same for the other two personas.

These three personas and descriptions make up your coat of arms.

---

**Step 8: Eric's Complete Coat of Arms**
I am a **Viking**; I move forward with determination and confidence. I lead through a strength of conviction, providing clarity of purpose for others, and together we make things happen.

I am a **Thriver;** I excel in any environment. I look forward to the challenges of the day and the excitement and variety they bring. If I can't find a way, I make a way!

I am a **Pioneer**; I think differently, creating new possibilities in an ever-changing environment.

---

**Congratulations!** You have completed your coat of arms. Remember, the purpose of this exercise is to tap into who you truly are: your True Self. The moments you selected offer insight into who you are, and what makes you unique. In times of indecision, remember to tap into who you truly are; it can change your life and help you overcome any challenge you may come up against.

## Why This Works

Our goal is to replace the old negative neuro-associations about ourselves that we've been developing over the years with new empowering associations (our coat of arms). By repeating our coat of arms on a daily basis (see your assignment at the end of this chapter), we build positive connections between our neurons, creating a super-highway delivering signals of conviction and empowerment.

The brain, like the body, works on the principle of 'use it or lose it'. Therefore, by not giving our old, disempowering thoughts any airtime, they will eventually die away, leaving only a sense of confidence in who we are.

## The Fear of Change

You may find that as you begin to change, there will be a little voice in your head pulling you back. This is your False Self, your old, comfortable self.

Caroline Myss, in her book *Sacred Contracts,* captures the sense of empowerment you feel when you experience your True Self: "When you do not seek or need external approval, you are at your most powerful. Nobody can disempower you emotionally or psychologically."

However, she goes on to warn that "change signals loss of control and entry into the unknown," and highlights the two reasons why people fear change.

1. People fear their own empowerment because it may cause us to separate from those who loved us for being vulnerable.
2. People fear change because we can no longer claim that we are not responsible for our actions.

The purpose of the False Self is to keep us safe, psychologically and emotionally. However, we cannot grow and become the person we wish to be by playing small.

Marianne Williamson captures this beautifully in her poem, 'Our Deepest Fear', from *A Return to Love*, made famous by Nelson Mandela when he used it in his 1994 inaugural speech.[1]

*Our deepest fear is not that we are inadequate.*
*Our deepest fear is that we are powerful beyond measure.*
*It is our light, not our darkness that most frightens us.*
*We ask ourselves, Who am I to be brilliant, gorgeous, talented,*
*fabulous?*
*Actually, who are you not to be?*
*You are a child of God.*
*Your playing small does not serve the world.*
*There is nothing enlightened about shrinking so that other people*
*won't feel insecure around you.*
*We are all meant to shine, as children do.*
*We were born to make manifest the glory of God that is within us.*
*It's not just in some of us; it's in everyone.*
*And as we let our own light shine, we unconsciously give other people*
*permission to do the same.*
*As we are liberated from our own fear, our presence automatically*
*liberates others.*

---

[1] Reprinted with permission

**Assignment**

Read your coat of arms aloud every morning, and consider deeply what it means to you. Think about your day ahead and how you want to show up, based on who you truly are.

In the evening, as you reflect on your day, notice what's changed, and how you're responding differently to situations that might have caused you to react rather than respond. Notice how you're becoming the better—truer—you.

## Coach's Tip

Jim Rohn is famous for saying, "Those things that are easy to do are also easy not to do." Here are a few suggestions from my clients to make sure you remember to read your coat of arms every morning:

- Set a recurring alarm on your phone
- Set a recurring calendar reminder
- Have it in your car and read it on the way to work
- Laminate it and keep it in the shower
- Have it next to your toilet!
- Tape it to your bathroom mirror.

What ways can you come up with to remember to read your coat of arms?

Now that you are beginning to know yourself a little more, a change is underway. And as in any change, there are always two forces at play: those that move us forward and those that hold us back. It's a little like driving a car with the brakes on.

Let's examine what might be holding you back.

# The Eagle That Couldn't Fly

*One day while on a walk in the mountains, a farmer found an abandoned eagle's nest. In it was an egg, still warm. He took the egg back to his farm and laid it in the nest of one of his hens. The egg hatched, and the baby eagle grew up along with the other chickens. It pecked about the farmyard, scrabbling for grain, spending its life in the yard and rarely looking up.*

*One day, the eagle, now very old, lifted its head and saw above it a wonderful sight—an eagle soaring high above in the sky. Looking at it, the old creature sighed and said to itself, "If only I'd been born an eagle."*

# CHAPTER 2

# The Power of Beliefs

*"I don't have the credibility to succeed."*

It's 6:58 a.m. on the morning of March 3rd, 2007. I'm sculling the water of Lake Taupo with my hands while I gently kick my legs behind me. I look around; all I can see are brightly coloured hats bobbing in the water, people jostling for position. There are over a thousand athletes waiting to begin; for most, it will be the longest day of their lives. In less than two minutes, a cannon will fire, signifying the start of the 22nd New Zealand Ironman. Ahead of us is a 3.8-kilometre swim, a 180-kilometre cycle, and a 42.2-kilometre run!

***

I had studied to be a fitness instructor when I was young, and had even entered a few triathlons. But though I had completed one (and it was the best feeling of my life), my accumulated injuries had kept me from finishing any more. Still, I would always get excited when a triathlon was on the television or when I would read an article about Ironman in a fitness magazine. Finally, my excitement piqued when I was flying from Australia to New Zealand while watching the highlights of the 2006 Western Australian Ironman event. What blew me away was the number of ordinary people crossing the finish line, people of all shapes and ages! That was it; I made up my mind there and then that I would complete an Ironman event.

The first thing I bought when I arrived in New Zealand was a pair of running shoes. I was determined, and nothing was going to stop me. I signed up for Ironman New Zealand, to be held in March 2007.

As I began my training, it wasn't long before old injuries made themselves known again. I had bursitis in my shoulder, runner's knee in both knees, and a hip that would explode in pain during moderate to long distances on the bike. Still, I found myself counting the seconds until the cannon sounded.

A few nervous moments later, we were off. The swim went pretty well, with my shoulder only flaring up near the end. I headed off on the bike, taking unhealthy amounts of Ibuprofen to quiet my aching hip and knees.

With the marathon run to go, I was completely spent. My body screamed, and I started considering giving up. I could just take off my race number and slip into the crowd; no one would ever really know. Besides, I reasoned, I gave it my best shot. My body just isn't up to this kind of thing.

I stopped at a drink station to rehydrate when I heard a voice behind me, asking for ice.

I turned around and saw a man sitting on the grass verge, taking off his second prosthetic limb. He had no legs below the knees, and the bandages on his left stump were bleeding.

He caught me staring, and smiled at me, giving me the thumbs up.

"Ironman," he said.

I ran on, but I couldn't get the athlete out of my mind. All of a sudden, my aches and pains weren't that bad. My thoughts of quitting turned to anger. I was angry at myself for being such a wimp!

As I looped around the run course and headed back toward Taupo, I saw the athlete running towards me. He was in obvious pain with every stride, but when he saw me coming, he smiled widely and put his hand up for a high five.

I ran towards him with my hand raised, but in my exhaustion, I completely missed—worst high five ever!

He kept on running, shouting, "Ironmannnnnn!"

I was so overcome with emotion that tears streamed down my face. At that moment, I had created a new belief! One that has stuck with me to this day.

Nothing is impossible; there is always a way. Always!

## It's Hard to Believe

Beliefs have a powerful effect on our decisions and our behaviours. The majority of people will stubbornly hold onto a belief even when there is little or no basis for it. Such beliefs may even be strengthened when others attempt to present evidence debunking them. This is a phenomenon known as the backfire effect.

For example, in a 2014 article in *The Atlantic*, journalist Cari Romm describes a study in which a group of people, concerned about the side effects of flu shots, became less willing to receive them after being told that the vaccination was entirely safe!

According to Lee Ross and Craig A. Anderson, "Beliefs are remarkably resilient in the face of empirical challenges that seem logically devastating."

Several experiments can be interpreted or re-interpreted with the aid of the belief perseverance concept. The first study of belief perseverance was carried out by Festinger, Riecken, and Schachter. These psychologists joined a cult whose members were convinced that the world would end on December 21, 1954. After the prediction failed, most believers still clung to their faith.

Well, they're whackos, you might reason. But here's another study that might baffle you about the power of beliefs.

Subjects spent about four hours following instructions of a hands-on instructional manual. At a certain point, the manual introduced a formula that incorrectly interpreted the volume of a particular sphere as 50 percent larger than it really was.

Subjects were then given an actual sphere and asked to determine its volume; first by using the formula, and then by filling the sphere with water, transferring the water to a box, and directly measuring the volume of the water in the box.

All nineteen subjects held a Ph.D. degree in a natural science, were employed as researchers or professors at two major universities, and carried out the comparison between the two volume measurements a second time with a larger sphere.

All but one of these scientists clung to the spurious formula despite their empirical observations.

## Understanding Beliefs

Henry Ford famously stated, "If you believe you can, you're right. If you believe you can't, you're right."

In fact, if we believe we can't do something, we probably won't even try. Therefore, our beliefs about ourselves and the world in general greatly impact our day-to-day effectiveness.

One of the most famous examples of why we shouldn't be constrained by our beliefs is the story of the four-minute mile. For years, it was thought that it was impossible for a human being to run a mile in less than four minutes. Then on May 6, 1954, Roger Bannister achieved the impossible. Within six weeks of Bannister shattering this belief, John Lundy took another second off Bannister's time. In the nine years following, nearly two hundred people broke through this seemingly impenetrable barrier.

Our beliefs influence nearly every aspect of our lives: our health, our intelligence, our creativity, our relationships, and our happiness. Just like the creation of the self, of which beliefs are a part of, many of our beliefs were instilled in us when we were children. We picked them up from our parents, media, friends, teachers, and other influential members of society that we were exposed to.

The great news is that if we picked them up, it means that they're made up; and if they're made up, we can change them!

## The Psychology of Beliefs

In his book *Sleight of Mouth*, Robert Dilts explains that, neurologically, beliefs are associated with the limbic system and the hypothalamus in the midbrain. The limbic system is the emotional part of the brain and doesn't understand fact or logic. That's why when we believe something deeply, no amount of logic can move us.

As well as regulating emotions, the limbic system is also associated with long-term memory and integrating information from the higher centres of the brain, the cortex, and the autonomic nervous system. Therefore, because beliefs are produced in the deeper structures of the brain, they trigger physiological changes in the body and are responsible for many of our unconscious responses. This is why we have a physiological response that can be picked up by a polygraph when we talk about something we believe to be untrue; for example, telling a lie.

Dilts goes on to explain that when we have a belief about something, we tend to behave in such a way that leads to the fruition of that belief.

"Beliefs," Dilts writes, "tend to have a self-organising or 'self-fulfilling' effect on our behaviour at many levels, focusing attention in one area and filtering it out of others."

## Beliefs That Hold Us Back

Dilts categorises the most common types of beliefs that hold us back in life as the following:

1. **Hopelessness** - The belief that, regardless of our capabilities, the goal is not achievable.
2. **Helplessness** - The belief that the goal is possible to achieve, but we are not capable of achieving it.
3. **Worthlessness** - The belief that we are undeserving of the goal because of something we have done.

To be successful, it is necessary to transform these beliefs into beliefs centering on "hope for the future, a sense of capability and responsibility, and a sense of self-worth and belonging." But if our beliefs are so ingrained in us and from such an early age, how do we change them?

## How to Transform a Limiting Belief

In his bestselling book *Awaken the Giant Within*, Anthony Robbins divides beliefs into three categories varying in emotion and intensity: opinions, beliefs, and convictions.

Opinions he likens to our cognitive tabletop, supported only by wobbly, unverified legs and therefore relatively easy to change. A belief, on the other hand, has several strong reference points that we can verify as fact... at least in our own minds. Lastly, a conviction surpasses a belief primarily because of the emotional intensity associated with the idea.

Let's use this analogy to demonstrate how a belief is formed and how we can dismantle a limiting belief. Then, let's create a new empowering belief, a belief that supports us and opens up new possibilities.

Figure 2-1 illustrates the opinion that 'All Irish people are dishonest.' Being Irish myself, I can see the funny side of this statement. This is supported by several references or supporting structures. Let's examine them individually:

- **Thieves** - My father worked with an Irishman on a building site once, and he didn't show up for work one day. It was later discovered that money had gone missing from the office drawer. Everyone knew he stole it.
- **Big drinkers** - It's common knowledge that the Irish like their drink. And you can't trust a people who are drunk all the time.
- **IRA** - It's also known that all Irish people are connected in some way to the IRA, and you can't trust a group like that.
- **Car** - My friend bought a car from an Irish guy once, who swore on his life it wouldn't give any trouble. Within three months, the car was constantly breaking down. It gave my friend nothing but trouble!

FIGURE 2-1

**A Belief is a Table Top with Legs (Supporting References)**

So now imagine the scenario where you're in a bar and a friend of yours introduces you to an Irish person. If you've got the belief that all Irish people are dishonest, it's going to influence your every interaction with this person—whom you don't even know. Later on in the evening, if someone says, "I've lost my mobile phone," where are your thoughts immediately going to go? As Dilts says, we're going to filter out other alternatives and quickly arrive at the conclusion… it's the Irish guy! He stole it.

If we want to change this belief, it's not enough to decide that 'All Irish people are honest,' because in our minds there are too many references to dispute that fact. To change a belief, first we must dismantle the references one by one; we must weaken the cognitive supporting structure of the belief.

How do we do this? We look for alternative evidence and challenge the reference.

So let's dismantle the belief by challenging the references.

- **Thieves** - My father worked with an Irishman on a building site once, and he didn't show up for work one day. It was later discovered that money had gone missing from the office desk. Everyone knew he stole it.

  I wonder if it's possible that the Irish guy got a new job across town with an immediate start or perhaps a family member got sick and he had to leave urgently. Perhaps the real thief spread rumours about the Irish guy because he wasn't there to defend himself. Perhaps he was completely innocent.

- **Big drinkers** - It's common knowledge that the Irish like their drink. You can't trust a people who are drunk all the time.

  In fact, although the Irish do like a drink or two, the country that consumes the most alcohol is Lithuania. The French and Germans consume more alcohol than the Irish. So are we saying that we can't trust the Germans, the French, the Lithuanians, the Austrians, and the Hungarians? Is alcohol consumption really a good measure of how trustworthy a people are?

- **IRA** - It's also known that all Irish people are connected in some way to the IRA, and you can't trust a group like that.

  There was a time in Irish history that led to the formation of the IRA to stand against the oppression of Irish people. However, those involved were a small minority. Most Irish people, like people of other nations, just want to raise a family in a safe and peaceful environment.

- **Car** - My friend bought a car from an Irish guy once, who swore on his life it wouldn't give any trouble. Within three months, the car was constantly breaking down. It gave my friend nothing but trouble!

  Perhaps the car was running beautifully when the guy sold it, and, after all, it is the buyer's responsibility to check the condition of the vehicle before purchase. Besides, it really is a bit of a stretch to say that the Irish have the monopoly on selling dodgy cars all over the world! Don't you think?

So there you have it. After shaking the reference legs of our cognitive table top, the belief doesn't hold any concrete supporting evidence. Maybe it's just true that some people are dishonest, regardless of their nationality.

### *Creating a New Empowering Belief*

If our beliefs are arbitrary and made up, that means we can create new beliefs—new beliefs that will support us and help us be the type of person we wish to be.

Using the tabletop metaphor, let's create a new empowering belief! "I'm soooo sexy!"

If I want to create the belief that I'm sexy, the first thing I have to do is create reference points to support that belief. So I look into my past and conjure up the evidence that authenticates that statement. Let's examine them individually:

- **Work out** - I work out and take care of my body. It's my opinion that anyone who looks after their body is sexy.
- **Jeans** - I look good in a pair of jeans. Anyone who looks good in a pair of jeans is sexy.
- **Ex-Girlfriend** - An ex-girlfriend of mine told me one time that I'm so sexy. Now, her words were a little slurred and she was a little unsteady on her feet, but I'll take it.
- **Car** - Lastly and most importantly, I drive a Nissan Blue Bird! It's silver, and that's a sexy color.

Even if I'm not particularly sexy, if I *perceive* that I'm physically attractive, it's going to change how I act and behave.

FIGURE 2-2

**Creating a New Empowering Belief**

According to Lorelle Burton, Drew Westen, and Robin Kowalski in Psychology, "Individuals who perceive themselves to be physically attractive report being more extroverted, socially comfortable and mentally healthy than those who are less comfortable with their appearance. Although they may be simply deluded in every realm of their lives, it is equally likely that seeing themselves as attractive produces a self-fulfilling prophecy, in which feeling attractive leads to behaviours perceived by others as attractive. In fact, research consistently finds that when people feel and act attractive, others are more likely to see them that way."

Therefore, if you have a particular belief about yourself, it's more likely that your behaviours and decision-making will reinforce this belief, adding more and more references until it becomes a conviction and undeniably true.

## Getting Personal

Here are a couple of disempowering beliefs I held onto for years, but had to break free from if I was ever going to be happy.

1. I'll never be accepted by the group.
2. I don't have the credibility to succeed.

When I acknowledge this first belief, it hit me hard. I immediately recognised how this belief was influencing my behaviour. I remember how I'd hang back a little from the group, how I wouldn't speak up or get involved. Sure enough, by my not interacting, my belief became a self-fulfilling prophecy. I became more withdrawn and unsure of myself.

When I decided to counter this belief, I looked for evidence in my past. And it wasn't long before I came up with several examples when I had felt a part of the group!

I realised that during those moments, I had been actively getting involved. I had introduced myself, started a conversation, or made a joke. This led to a new empowering belief:

**'When I'm around other people, and I make the effort, I will always be accepted.'**

The second limiting belief shook me to my bones because, at the time, I was about to start my own leadership coaching business. I remember sharing this belief with my friend and amazing coach, Moira Mallon. Who is going to want coaching from me? I've never held a C-level position. Who am I to coach anyone?

Moira listened patiently, as she always did. She looked me directly in the eye and said, "Cillín, it's your passion that will get you through."

I held onto this shaky supporting reference for months, until I got my first client, and then my next, and then my next. Slowly, I built stronger and stronger references, until that belief was well and truly shattered!

So what's my new belief?

**'I'm blessed to be able to positively impact people's lives.'**

On the flip side, there are four enduring beliefs that I use to guide my decisions when I'm around people, find myself in a conflict situation, or up against an obstacle:

1. People do the best that they can with the resources available to them.
2. Every communication is either a loving response or a cry for help.
3. There is always a way!
4. You haven't yet met the person who will change your life.

These beliefs have strongly influenced the direction of my life over the years, and have encouraged me to be bold, courageous, and above all, to be gentle.

---

**Assignment**

Now that you understand a little more about the power of beliefs, how are your beliefs holding you back? What are the beliefs that empower you?

Grab your notebook, and at the top of a blank page, write Disempowering Beliefs. On another page, write Empowering Beliefs.

Now, let's brainstorm all those beliefs that hold you back in your life and all those beliefs that move you forward, proud to be who you are!

You can use the following categories to get you started:

- People
- Your workplace
- Yourself
- Your family
- Time
- Money
- Scarcity or abundance
- Your abilities
- Your physical body

Let's focus on shattering your limiting beliefs now!

---

***Live your beliefs and you can turn the world around***
~ Henry David Thoreau

On top of a clean sheet of paper, write down the first belief you'd like to change.

Now, with this belief in mind, write down the answers to these questions:

1. How could the opposite of this belief be true? What evidence do I have to demonstrate this belief is ridiculous or absurd?

2. What is the positive intention behind this belief? How is it serving me? How can I get what I want, but leave behind the limitations of carrying this belief?

3. Was the person I learned this belief from a good role model in this area?

4. What will it cost me in my relationships, my health, my finances, and my loved ones if I don't let go of this belief? In ten or twenty years, what will my life be like if I don't let go of this belief now?

Now, what's a new belief you have that will replace this old belief? Write it down, and underneath it write down as many supporting references as you can. Ask yourself, how does this belief empower me? Or, how <u>could</u> this belief empower me?

Next, take your top three empowering beliefs and write down as many supporting references as you can think of. Go deep and create as many reference legs to your cognitive table top as you can.

## Coach's Tip

Along with your coat of arms, review your new empowering beliefs daily, until they become so ingrained in you that you act and think in ways that are congruent with who you are and who you are becoming.

If you've completed the exercises in the last two chapters, you may have found a deeper awareness of yourself. We're going to go even deeper now to ensure you are always heading in the right direction.

# Wisdom in a Cup

*A group of former university students, highly established in their careers, got together to visit their old university professor. Soon their conversations turned to complaints about stress in work and life. The professor, upon offering his guests coffee, went to the kitchen and returned with a large pot of coffee and an assortment of cups: plastic, glass, crystal, some plain, some expensive, and some quite exquisite. Setting down the tray, the professor tells the students to help themselves to the coffee.*

*When all the students had a cup of coffee in their hand, the professor said, "If you noticed, all the nice looking, expensive cups were taken up, leaving behind the plain and cheap ones. While it is normal for you to want only the best for yourselves, that is the source of your problems and stress. Be assured that the cup itself adds no quality to the coffee. In most cases, it is just more expensive, and in some cases it even hides what we drink. What all of you really wanted was coffee, not the cup, but you subconsciously went for the best cups... And then you began eying each other's cups.*

*"Now consider this," he continued. "Life is the coffee; the jobs, money, and your positions in society are the cups. They are just tools to hold and contain life, and the type of cup we have does not define us, nor change the quality of the life we live. Sometimes, by*

*concentrating only on the cup, we fail to enjoy the coffee that has been provided us."*

*He paused to allow this to sink in. "Nature brews the coffee, not the cups. Enjoy your coffee!"*

# CHAPTER 3

# Your True North

*The answer for Sarah wasn't in setting a new goal.*

My wife and I were dating for about ten years before we decided we would tie the knot at a beautiful, 19th-century gothic castle called Kinnitty Castle in the heart of the Slieve Bloom Mountains in County Offaly, Ireland. It was a date to remember, because not only did we get married on March 18th—the day after St Patrick's Day—it was also the day Ireland was playing England at Twickenham for the Triple Crown!

The invites were sent, the dress was bought, and everything was going according to plan when I got the phone call.

"I'm sorry, man. I can't come to your wedding."

These were the words from one of my best friends. I couldn't believe it… I was pretty upset at the news, and went through every solution I could think of to have him and his wife attend. You see, my best friend recently had a little girl. He and his wife didn't want to be away from home overnight, and he didn't want to be away from his new family even for one night.

I never questioned his friendship, but I couldn't fully understand how he could make this decision and know, for him and his family, it was the right one. That is, until I learned about value systems.

Flicking through the news articles of the day, it doesn't take long to come across a story or two where the underlying cause of people's behaviour is demonstrated by a lack of values. At the time of writing, the #MeToo campaign is in full swing, and women and men are speaking up against sexual harassment, not only in Hollywood but also in workplaces and society in general. Rightly so, as no one should have to put up with being assaulted or pressured into doing something that makes them feel uncomfortable.

Speaking at the Oxford Union in England in 2017, Ian McKellen is quoted as saying, "From my own experience, when I was starting acting in the early '60s, the director of the theatre I was working at showed me some photographs he got from women who were wanting jobs... some of them had at the bottom of their photograph the letters DRR—*directors' rights respected*. In other words, if you give me a job, you can have sex with me."

What is it that causes a Harvey Weinstein to think that it's okay to swap sexual favours for casting women in movie roles? What is it that causes the women who want acting jobs to write DRR on their photographs and, if what McKellan is saying is true, exchange sex for jobs?

The answer lies in our value system. But what is a value, and how does it influence our behaviour?

According to the Oxford Dictionary, value refers to "the importance, worth, or usefulness of something". Simply put, a value is something that is important to us. We have values for every aspect of our lives; we have values around our health, our relationships, our finances, our careers, and so on.

For this book, we're going to focus on personal values; these largely encompass who you are as a person and what's important to you.

Values and beliefs are, of course, closely aligned, but they influence our lives in different ways. Our values, whether we're aware of them or not, are inherent in every choice we make. They are at the heart of the criteria we use to make decisions. In fact, if you've ever struggled to make an important life decision, it's likely that you were unclear about your values. Values are also a major factor in evaluating what we have done. For example, if we do something that is not aligned with our value system, we feel a sense of guilt about taking that action. Guilt is the brain's way of letting us know we've gone off track.

Similar to beliefs, our values were instilled in us at an early age. Which means that like beliefs, they're made up! Therefore, if there's any aspect of your life that you're not happy with, you can change it. Change your value system and you change your life.

## The Relationship Between Values and Beliefs

The United States has never had such polarising views of past and present presidencies as it does today. You might think that I'm going out on a limb here when I say that both Obama and Trump have at least one value in common—to keep America safe. In this instance, it's not the value that's the issue, but the belief of how to achieve this value.

Obama believes that keeping America safe should be done through negotiation, collaboration, and respect for other nations and cultures. Trump, on the other hand, believes that building a wall and targeting certain Muslim-based countries for exclusion is the way to go. The value is the same, but their beliefs about how to achieve it are quite different. Our beliefs support the execution of our values.

Because values are expressed in general terms such as family, money, success, etc., it's difficult to pin down the meaning behind them. Therefore, to better understand our values, we must get more specific about what they mean to us. As in the example above, both presidents value safety, but it means a very different thing in terms of behaviour and execution.

## A Source of Motivation

Those things that we find important, worthy or useful are things that we tend to want more of in life. Therefore, our values are a primary source of motivation for us. In fact, our goals in life are a manifestation of our values.

In my early adult years, I was very ambitious, and that ambition drove me to work ridiculously hard, holding down a full-time job as well as two other part-time jobs while going to school! I also set up small side businesses. I was so driven to succeed in my twenties, it was all I could think about. How to make money! Not only was I working hard (and not really working smart), but I got to the point where I lost my motivation. I didn't know why or how it happened, but I just settled into a nine-to-five job and started living life like a 'normal' person.

I like to think I know a little more about myself now. Back in my twenties, the meaning of success for me was about having stuff—the nice car, the house, the holidays, all the things money can buy. So much so that I neglected all the other areas of my life. I never took holidays, because I was too busy 'achieving'.

Success means many things to many people, but isn't it true that success is a little broader than having the things that money can buy? Success has a different meaning for me now; it's more about improving my life in all the areas that are important to me. Constantly improving my relationship with my wife and daughters, improving and maintaining my health and well-being, and learning and growing through areas of study that interest me. And yes, improving my financial situation, but doing it through the things I love to do.

As long as I'm improving in those areas of life, I feel pretty successful. That feeling of progress can be expressed by the word

Kaizen, the Japanese word for 'constant improvement'. Many industries that focus on lean production and a philosophy of constant improvement have adopted Kaizen as their default way of working.

So where did all that motivation that I had in my twenties go? Some might say, "Well, you got a little older and realised there are other more important things in life than money," or "You burned yourself out and got smart about a few things."

Maybe... but I think it has more to do with the two powerful psychological forces that shape our lives: *Moving Toward* motivation and *Moving Away From* motivation... the principles of pain and pleasure.

### Moving Towards Motivation

Moving towards motivation, also referred to as performance-approach goals, motivates us to achieve an outcome, meet a certain standard, and feel pleasure. Being driven to study hard for an exam to achieve an A grade is an example of moving towards motivation. Another would be learning a skill or performing at a particular level, such as skiing a black diamond slope.

### Moving Away From Motivation

Moving away from motivation, also known as performance-avoidance goals, motivates us to avoid disappointment or embarrassment. Expanding on the examples above, rather than face the humiliation of failing an exam, I might study hard to avoid a C grade. I might also prefer to remain on the easier ski slopes to avoid the embarrassment of sliding down the tougher slopes on my backside. In both cases, I would be avoiding the emotional pain I believed would come with a perceived failure. However, the first example is about learning and growing, and the other is about avoiding.

Looking back over the years, I think my motivation stemmed from my experience travelling around Australia and New Zealand when I was younger. I didn't plan things very well; I pretty much bummed my way around the place and ended up travelling back to Ireland through America on a wing and a prayer!

I remember thinking that <u>I never want to experience that again in my life</u>, and that was my motivation for having money. I wanted all the things life could offer, and <u>never have to worry about how I was going to survive</u>.

But that's the problem with moving away from motivation. As soon as I got comfortable—a nice car, money in the bank, living in a nice apartment and a reasonably well-paying job—my motivation started to fall away. I stopped creating goals and started to drift from one day to the next.

Therefore, once you determine what you want, it's important to understand your motivations for achieving it. Ask yourself: "How do I know when I have success?" "What does that look like?" and "What causes me to feel successful?"

Listen to the answers, and if there are any negative statements (see my underlined statements above) or statements of necessity (should, must, have to, etc.), it's likely that there is an element of moving away from motivation in your reasoning for having something. Often, your reasoning will be a combination of moving towards motivations and moving away from motivations, so pay attention. This is what might be preventing you from reaching your full potential in life.

### Mastery Motivation

Both moving towards and moving away from motivation are about achieving an outcome, either through gaining pleasure or avoiding pain. Mastery motivation, on the other hand, is the motivation to increase one's mastery of a skill. People who are motivated by mastery are interested in developing their skill or technique, not by the pleasure of success or by the pain of failure. They are consumed by the practice itself, which can be both painful and pleasurable at different levels of skill acquisition.

The research indicates that children with a moving towards motivation focus gain good grades, but they may or may not develop an intrinsic interest in the material. For them, it is about achieving the grade. Students with a moving away from motivation style tend to get low grades and derive less intrinsic pleasure from their studies. Lastly, children motivated by mastery tend to get good grades *and* develop intrinsic interest in the study material.

Check in with yourself for a moment. Are you pursuing the things that are important to you in life to avoid pain or to gain pleasure? Or are you pursuing them for the mastery?

*Desire is the key to motivation, but it's the determination and commitment to unrelenting pursuit of your goal—a commitment to excellence—that will enable you to attain the success you seek.*
~ Mario Andretti

## Values in Conflict

Angela is an effective team leader who has a strong moving toward motivation quality. She has done a good job hiring the right people, and everything is going great in her department. The team gets on, pulls their weight, and they are all performing well. Then a restructure occurs, and a couple of people—whom Angela would not have hired herself—end up on her team.

Angela does everything right. She makes a big deal of welcoming them to the team, ensures they have everything they need to perform their roles, spends time getting to know them, etc. However, no matter what she tries, they just don't seem to be pulling their weight. The rest of the team starts to complain that the quality of their work is poor and they have to take up the slack.

Although Angela reiterates the importance of quality to the new team members, this has little effect, and things don't change. Eventually, the rest of the team stops picking up the slack, and the team results suffer. Previously loyal team members look for other positions within the organisation or leave altogether.

One of Angela's core moving towards values is quality, and she hired the right people to ensure this value became a team value. However, there is a moving away value that is at play here also. It is the fear of conflict, something that Angela avoids at any cost... even to the detriment of her team. This isn't an uncommon scenario in leadership roles, and it often causes huge internal discomfort.

It's true for the rest of us too. Always meeting our values is a tough task. We all have values we move toward and values we move away from, and at times we may feel like there is an internal struggle between the two.

## *Understanding the Internal Struggle*

As a kid growing up, one of my favourite cartoon characters was Donald Duck. You just knew that no matter how happy he was at the beginning of the cartoon, things were going to go terribly wrong. He always ended up getting the short end of the stick... largely of his own making.

I always liked when Donald hit a moral dilemma (values conflict), and sure enough, a little devil would appear on his right shoulder, encouraging him to go after what he wanted regardless of the consequences. Then, of course, a little angel would appear on his left, pleading with him to do the right thing.

Have you ever tried to make sense of that internal struggle? We all have!

Freud's theory of psychology explains the workings of the self through the relationship between the id, the superego, and the ego.

Allow me to introduce you to that little devil on your shoulder... the id... and why leaving this little fella unchecked is bad for leadership.

According to Freud, the id is the original source of drive energy. Referred to as the 'great reservoir' of mental energy, the id is very basic in its function. Its sole purpose is to release excitation and tension. It needs to get rid of that pent up frustration so we can return to a quiet internal state... calm and relaxed.

The id also operates according to the pleasure principle, and so pursues pleasure and avoids pain. It wants what it wants when it wants it! It's the personification of the spoiled child. The id has no concept of moral value or consequences, and operates entirely at the unconscious level, which makes it a tricky bugger.

Lastly, the id achieves its goal for immediate gratification in one of two ways: taking action or through imagination. This is an important distinction when it comes to goal accomplishment. Research tells us that a high percentage of people may have goals, but rather than taking action, they imagine what it would be like to have attained the goal. This gives them enough of a sense of satisfaction to never take the steps necessary to actually achieve it!

> ### *The ego is not master in its own house.*
> ~ Sigmund Freud

Conversely, on the other shoulder is the little angel... the superego. The superego represents the moral aspects of social behaviour. It contains the ideals we all strive for and keeps us aligned with those ethical standards laid down by society. Ultimately, the superego is an internal representation of the moral rules (values) in our external social world. It controls our behaviour through emotional rewards. If our behaviour is aligned with our or society's morals, we are rewarded with positive emotions such as pride or self-love; we hear that praise we all crave. If we deviate from our moral code, we are punished with the emotions of guilt or feelings of inferiority; guilt is a big one for the superego—our parents have trained us well!

The superego operates at a relatively primitive level of the mind. It operates in line with the perfection principle, and expresses itself in terms of black-and-white thinking, making all-or-none judgements. There's no room for negotiation; that's good or that's bad, that's right or that's wrong. It is incapable of reality testing, and can therefore be quite inflexible in its approach to solving real-world problems. Being this inflexible also places a constraint on a leader's ability to get things done.

Lastly, there's the ego. When Freud coined the term ego, he didn't mean it to mean, 'Look at the big ego on that guy.' The ego seeks out reality. Its function is to express and satisfy the desires of the id while balancing the demands of the superego and real-world opportunities and constraints. Based on the reality principle, the ego wants to maximise pleasure and minimise pain (or negative consequences), and it achieves this by blocking, diverting, or gradually releasing the energy of the id while meeting the demands of reality and the superego. It's got a tough job! Unlike the superego and the id, the ego can compromise through rational thought, it can distinguish reality from fantasy, and it is capable of tolerating tension.

Therefore to successfully navigate through the challenges life throws at us, we need a strong ego!

## Coach's Tip

To develop your ego strength, and hence your ability to be true to your values, here are a few things you can work on:
- Acceptance of yourself—warts and all. Know that we are all perfect in our own way and we are all on a journey. Keep working on your coat of arms and getting to know your True Self.

- Train yourself to take a wider perspective on things. Examine your personal rules about the different aspects of your life, such as rules about yourself, other people, relationships, fairness, and life in general (we'll explore these in detail in the next chapter).

- Take back your power! Take responsibility for your thoughts, your words, and your actions. Increase your sense of efficacy in the areas of life that are important to you. Be proactive, actively practice resourcefulness, and take action!

- Develop an attitude of flexibility. Be accepting of and open to change… because everything changes! Be mindful of the meanings you attach to events and experiences; do you default to negative or positive when something happens? Often, this simple change in perspective can make all the difference (we'll show you how to do this in the next section).

A strong ego is necessary for solid leadership.

*The ego is only an illusion, but a very influential one. Letting the ego-illusion become your identity can prevent you from knowing your true self. Ego, the false idea of believing that you are what you have or what you do, is a backwards way of assessing and living life.*
~ Wayne Dyer

## Determining Your Values

Any hill walker or pioneer will tell you that one of the most important pieces of equipment you can have is a compass. Regardless of visibility, if you have a compass, you always know what direction you're headed. The same is true for life. If you have clarity of your values, you always know where your true north is. That's why our values are so important; they give us direction. Our values act as our personal compass. So let's determine your values now!

---

**Determining Your Values**

Step 1: On a Post-it Note, answer this question: **What's most important to me in life?** Values tend to be one-word descriptors, such as love, freedom, success, or friendship. If you get stuck, you can draw from the list of values in Figure 3-1. Five words is a good number to get you started.

Now, look at your values. They're likely to be moving toward values, the things you want more of. Put these aside for the moment.

Step 2: On a separate Post-it Note, answer this question: **What are the emotions (moving away from values) I avoid?** Again, these tend to be one-word descriptors: fear, rejection, anger, conflict, humiliation.

Repeat this exercise until you have highlighted all the emotional states you tend to move away from. As Freud says, "Being entirely honest with oneself is a good exercise."

Well done! You now have a list of your moving towards values and your moving away from values (or emotions that cause you pain). Let's reconcile these.

---

*When your values are clear to you, making decisions becomes easier.*
~ Roy E. Disney

FIGURE 3-1

**Life Values**

| | | |
|---|---|---|
| Abundance | Empathy | Preparedness |
| Acceptance | Energy | Presence |
| Accountability | Enjoyment | Privacy |
| Accuracy | Enthusiasm | Proactivity |
| Achievement | Excellence | Professionalism |
| Acknowledgement | Excitement | Prosperity |
| Activeness | Expertise | Prudence |
| Adaptability | Exploration | Punctuality |
| Adventure | Fairness | Rationality |
| Affection | Family | Realism |
| Affluence | Fearlessness | Recreation |
| Altruism | Fidelity | Reflection |
| Appreciation | Fitness | Relaxation |
| Approachability | Flexibility | Reliability |
| Audacity | Freedom | Reputation |
| Awareness | Friendship | Resilience |
| Beauty | Fun | Resourcefulness |
| Being the best | Generosity | Respect |
| Benevolence | Gratitude | Responsibility |
| Bravery | Growth | Sacrifice |
| Calmness | Happiness | Security |
| Camaraderie | Health | Self-control |
| Candour | Honesty | Selflessness |
| Care | Honour | Self-reliance |
| Challenge | Humility | Self-respect |
| Change | Humour | Sensitivity |
| Charity | Independence | Sensuality |
| Cheerfulness | Individuality | Serenity |
| Commitment | Influence | Service |

| | | |
|---|---|---|
| Community | Ingenuity | Sharing |
| Compassion | Insightfulness | Shrewdness |
| Competence | Inspiration | Significance |
| Competition | Integrity | Simplicity |
| Completion | Intelligence | Sincerity |
| Composure | Intimacy | Skilfulness |
| Confidence | Justice | Spirituality |
| Congruency | Kindness | Spontaneity |
| Connection | Leadership | Status |
| Consistency | Learning | Strength |
| Contentment | Liveliness | Success |
| Contribution | Love | Support |
| Conviction | Loyalty | Teamwork |
| Cooperation | Marriage | Thrift |
| Courage | Mastery | Timeliness |
| Courtesy | Mindfulness | Tranquillity |
| Creativity | Modesty | Transcendence |
| Credibility | Motivation | Trust |
| Curiosity | Nature | Understanding |
| Decisiveness | Open-mindedness | Valour |
| Determination | Outrageousness | Variety |
| Discipline | Patience | Virtue |
| Discovery | Passion | Vision |
| Discretion | Peace | Vitality |
| Diversity | Perfection | Warmth |
| Dynamism | Perseverance | Wealth |
| Education | Persuasiveness | Winning |

*Education without values, as useful as it is, seems rather to make man a more clever devil.*

~ C. S. Lewis

# Values hierarchy

Sarah was a client of mine who wanted to lose weight. Once we explored her 'why' behind her desire to lose the weight, we focused on creating a plan to help her achieve her goal. But something was troubling her. Sarah shared that she had achieved her target weight a couple of times in the past, but inevitably she ended up putting it all back on again. What she wanted to know was how she could keep it off permanently.

I asked her what her pattern was once she achieved her weight loss goal in the past. She explained that when she achieved her target weight, she celebrated by eating whatever she wanted and enjoyed looking fabulous in her new 'reward' clothes. She would exercise for a while after that, but soon other things like family, work, friends, etc., would take priority. Then, pound by pound, the weight would slowly creep back on until she was back to her old uncomfortable weight.

## *The Thermostat Effect*

A thermostat is a simple device that detects the temperature of a room. It can be set at different levels, so that when the temperature in the room drops to a certain level, the thermostat will trigger the heat to come on. As the temperature in the room rises and reaches a certain level, the thermostat triggers the heat to turn off again. And so it goes.

Sarah's pattern is similar to the thermostat. We don't only react in this way to our weight; we react this way in many areas of our lives: our weight, our relationships, our careers, and our finances! How many times have we heard of someone being in a great relationship—but then bam! They start to behave in ways that sabotage it. This is another example of a values conflict... *I'm falling in love, but I've been in love before and then I got hurt really badly, so I better make sure that doesn't happen again!*

Or how many Lotto millionaires out there have lost their wealth within a few years of winning it?

This pattern is the all too familiar one of pain (away from) and pleasure (towards). For Sarah, the pain of not being able to fit into her clothes triggers a change in her motivation. She diets and exercises hard, and sure enough, her weight starts to come down and she feels the pleasure of achieving her goal. But because she's motivated by pain, once the pain goes away, so does the motivation, and her weight starts to creep up again until the pain becomes too great... and so on. The answer for Sarah wasn't in setting a new goal. The answer was in understanding her values hierarchy.

Understanding your values hierarchy is important, because our values heavily influence our decisions. When they come into conflict, knowing which values are most important to us will help us make the right decision.

For example, Figure 3-2 represents Sarah's original values hierarchy. Looking at these, it's clear to see the forces at play here. Health in her moving towards values is ranked seventh, which means

Figure 3-2

**Sarah's Original Values Hierarchy**

it gets relegated down in importance if something more important, like relationships, family, or career comes along. This is, of course, until the emotional pain she associates with being overweight becomes too great.

## Who Do You Want To Be?

Our values shape our destiny. Remember that our values are instilled in us at an early age, and because they're made up, we can change them.

Therefore, if you change your values, you will change your life. You'll make new decisions. Decisions that help move you in the direction you want to go. Figure 3-3 represents Sarah's new moving towards value hierarchy.

Figure 3-3

**Sarah's New Values Hierarchy**

As you can see, she decided to give more of a focus in her life to health and energy. This way, she reasoned, she would be more fun to be around. Her friendships are still important to her, and she has since organised a walking group with her friends and has gym dates with others. This way she gets to meet these three values at the same time. Sarah's career is still important to her, but by focusing on her personal growth, her passion for what she does and having fun at work (imagine that as a concept!), life for Sarah is so much more enjoyable.

---

**Creating your values hierarchy**
Starting at the bottom of your list of values, ask yourself, "**Is X more important than Y, or is Y more important than X?**" Change the ordering of the values as necessary. Repeat this all the way up your hierarchy until they are in the right order.

Now check to see if each value supports the one above it. Does it feel right?

---

## A Means to an End

So often, people pursue their values through goals, and end up feeling empty, asking the question, "Is this all there is?" What they

Figure 3-4

**Means Values and End Values**

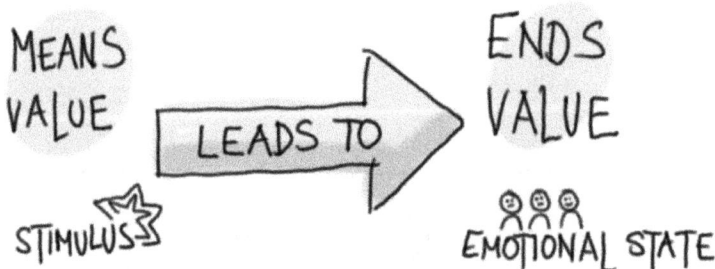

MEANS VALUE — STIMULUS — LEADS TO — ENDS VALUE — EMOTIONAL STATE

are failing to realise is that there are two categories of values: *means values* and *ends values* (Figure 3-4). Means values are those things in our lives that are important to us. They trigger an emotional state. However, to be fulfilled in life, we need to focus on ends values. End values produce results.

After considering Sarah's ends values, let's look at Sarah's new hierarchy. Taking Sarah through the exercises that follow, this is what her final values hierarchy looked like (Figure 3-5).

*I have learned that as long as I hold fast to my beliefs and values—and follow my own moral compass—then the only expectations I need to live up to are my own.*
~ Michelle Obama

Figure 3-5

**Sarah's Ends Values**

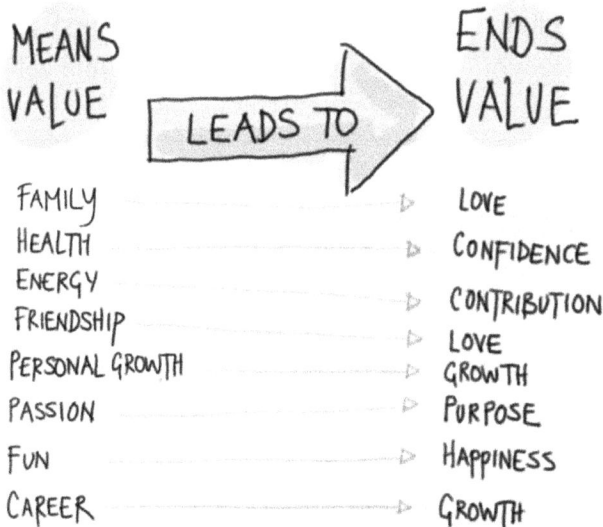

| MEANS VALUE | LEADS TO | ENDS VALUE |
|---|---|---|
| FAMILY | | LOVE |
| HEALTH | | CONFIDENCE |
| ENERGY | | CONTRIBUTION |
| FRIENDSHIP | | LOVE |
| PERSONAL GROWTH | | GROWTH |
| PASSION | | PURPOSE |
| FUN | | HAPPINESS |
| CAREER | | GROWTH |

Looking at Sarah's ends values, she achieves love through family and friends and confidence through feeling fit and healthy. When she has high energy, she can give more of herself to her family, her friends, and her personal growth. Sarah achieves personal growth through her own personal interests and her career. Her passion gives her a sense of purpose, and having fun gives her happiness.

Understanding the difference between means and ends values is vital to having a fulfilled and rewarding life. If love is what we're after, we can achieve this through many avenues. The same goes for confidence, contribution, and growth.

Let's discover your ends values.

---

**Creating your Ends Values**

For each of your values, ask this question: **"What do you get through having 'X' that's even more important?"** Another way of asking this question is: **"What does 'X' give you?"**

Do this for each of your values.

Congratulations! You have determined your new values hierarchy and have taken the first step in shaping your destiny!

Make sure you jot these down in notebook and refer to them often.

---

*With the right people, culture, and values, you can accomplish great things.*
~ Tricia Griffith

Now that you've assessed the direction of your life through your values, how do you know you're meeting them on a daily basis? Let's explore a strategy to help you stay on track.

# Another Lesson...

*The young monk and older monk were surprised during their walk by a maiden who approached for help crossing the stream that flowed before them. The younger monk immediately looked to the ground and did not respond.*

*The older monk, without hesitation, picked up the maiden in his arms and carried her across the stream to the opposite bank. There he placed her on her feet, and the two monks continued on their journey.*

*Just as they were a few minutes from arriving at their destination, the younger monk, clearly exasperated, turned to his colleague and asked, "How could you do that? All of our teachings strictly forbid any contact with the opposite sex!"*

*"I left the young woman by the bank of the stream," responded the older monk. "Are you still carrying her?"*

# CHAPTER 4

# Personal Rules

*I will never buy new clothes when I'm out of shape.*

A very close friend of mine, Pádraig, was celebrating the christening of his daughter. Louise, my then-girlfriend and now long-suffering wife, and I were invited back to his place to continue the celebrations. Pádraig and I first became friends when we met as fitness instructors at a gym in Dublin. I left the industry, but Pádraig went on to become one of the foremost fitness experts in Ireland, lecturing in Trinity College and having a starring role in a long-running and successful television programme called *The Health Squad*.

Now. as you can imagine at an Irish christening, there was a large spread of delicious food. Cakes, muffins, biscuits, pastries… it seemed endless! Unfortunately for me, I was on a bit of a diet, which largely consisted of no junk or sugary foods.

"Go on, have a bite." Louise held up a banoffee pie. "It's got a chocolate chip base, and it's so delicious," she teased. I was really struggling, counting down the minutes until the suffering would end.

At that moment, the proud father, Pádraig, saw what was going on and came over. He asked why I wasn't eating anything. I explained that since getting an office job, I was letting myself go a little and wanted to get back into shape.

He nodded in agreement. "I understand," he said. "I watch what I eat too. In fact, only if I work out really hard every day and watch what I eat during the week will I allow myself two biscuits after dinner on a Friday evening."

I was waiting for the wry smile that signified he was having me on, but it didn't come. Two biscuits!

I didn't know it at the time, but what Pádraig was articulating were his personal rules for health. Personal rules are similar to beliefs, but closer to the surface than our unconscious beliefs. We have them for every aspect of our lives. We have rules around our relationships, communication, how we drive, what we wear, our bodies, timekeeping, happiness… the list is endless. They act like shortcuts in the brain and tell us what's good and bad, what's right and what's wrong. Our personal rules enable us to make snap decisions about situations, people, and ourselves.

## The Problem with Rules

Our personal rules can be helpful, but they are a double-edged sword and can also lead to misery. Conversely, understanding our rules and formulating them in a positive and meaningful way can lead to a life of happiness and fulfilment.

Sometimes, people put themselves under tremendous pressure that can lead to unnecessary stress because of their personal rules. Examples might include:

I *must* be perfect.

Everyone *must* always appreciate me.

My meetings *must* always go smoothly.

Other people *must* always support my initiatives.

Albert Ellis, one of the pioneers of modern psychology, labelled this kind of thinking as unrealistic personal rules, or 'musterbations'; i.e., things we feel we must do because they are part of our Ought Self, or even just irrational thoughts that go unchallenged.

In his book *Practical Counselling and Helping Skills*, Richard Nelson-Jones lists several perceptual errors that can be caused by unrealistic personal rules.

- **Tunnel vision** - Focusing on only a portion of the available information regarding a problem rather than taking into account all significant data.

- **Magnifying and minimising** - Magnifying or exaggerating the qualities and significance of other people and events, or minimising them.

- **Negativeness** - Overemphasising negative aspects of people and yourself and minimising positive aspects. Always searching for weaknesses rather than for strengths. Applying negative labels to yourself and others, for example, 'I'm a loser' or 'My boss is impossible.'

- **Selective inattention** - Overlooking or being inattentive to material that may cause you anxiety. Denying and distorting information through defensive thinking.

- **Overgeneralising** - Making sweeping generalisations unsupported by evidence: 'All my meetings go swimmingly' or 'My work colleagues never stick to the point.'

- **Catastrophising** - Making highly negative predictions unsupported by evidence: 'My first day at my new job didn't go well, so I'm not going to do well in this organisation.'

- **Polarised thinking** - Perceiving in either/or and black-and-white terms (an over-developed superego): 'Either work colleagues are very cooperative or very uncooperative.'

- **Self-rating** - Going beyond functional ratings of specific characteristics to devaluing yourself as a whole person: 'I'm having difficulty influencing my colleagues. Therefore, I'm worthless.'

- **Mind reading** - Believing you can tell what people think without having collected adequate evidence or checked your conclusions.

As you can imagine, this type of thinking tends to spiral downward. It can only lead to emotional pain, for the person with these rules and those around them. As leaders, it's important for us to be aware of these rules in ourselves and in others. Ellis categorises unhelpful personal rules into three categories.

1. I *must* do well and win approval for all my performances.
2. Others *must* treat me considerately and kindly.
3. Conditions under which I live *must* be arranged so that I get practically everything I want comfortably, quickly and easily.

Nelson-Jones goes on to list some of the main characteristics of unrealistic or self-oppressing personal rules. You may recognise some of them in others… or even yourself.

- **Demandingness** - Thinking of things you want or desire as demands rather than preferences.
- **Perfectionism** - Putting pressure on yourself and others to be perfect. The reality is, nobody's perfect.
- **Self-rating** - Rating your self-worth based on accomplishments or how well you do performing a task.
- **Awfulising** - Thinking it is absolutely awful if you, others, or the environment are not as they should be.

We'll discuss how to deal with unrealistic personal rules that lead to stress and other unresourceful emotions in Part 2, when we delve into resilience and how to overcome adversity.

## The Flip Side

Psychologists tend to think of personal rules as unhealthy standards by which people judge themselves, largely consisting of 'musts', 'oughts', and 'shoulds'; however, there is more to personal rules than this. Anthony Robbins, in *Awaken the Giant Within*, sees rules as empowering. He reframes our personal rules as personal standards that we can consciously create to support our values.

Remember the question we asked at the end of the last chapter, 'How do you know that you're meeting these [values] on a daily basis?' Personal rules are the answer.

Rules can be divided into *Must Rules* and *Should Rules,* and how we perceive both can have a major impact on our health and happiness. Must Rules relate to our highest standards; they are important to us and must not be broken. Breaking our Must Rules will inevitably lead to emotional upset or anger.

Should Rules, on the other hand, are less important. Should Rules should be followed, but compromising on them from time to time will unlikely lead to an emotional reaction.

Pádraig, for example, has clear Must Rules for his health and physical body, and his body reflects that of someone with very high standards; he is in great shape. If Pádraig missed a workout during the week or ate poorly, how do you think he would react? Is he likely to brush it off as a one-time thing, or is he more likely to mentally beat himself up, doubling his efforts the following day?

Because Pádraig has clear Must Rules about his health, he's probably going to double down the next day, working twice as hard or being extra diligent with his diet.

A mutual friend of ours, Damian, also has rules about his health and physical body. However, Damian's rules about this aspect of his life are Should Rules. Damian knows he should work out at least three times a week; he knows he shouldn't eat that packet of biscuits after dinner; he knows he should stop eating that cake when he's stuffed...

But he rationalises to himself: "There's plenty of time to get into shape," "I'm going to enjoy the moment," "The great thing about Mondays is that they signify new beginnings... I'll start then."

As you can imagine, Damian has the physical appearance of someone who has Should Rules for his health and physical body.

I recognise that I've got clear Must Rules about my physical body, but they're not as stringent as Pádraig's, or as loose as Damian's. As a general example, one rule I have is that I will never buy new clothes when I'm out of shape, because that's the start of a slippery slope. My clothes act as the trigger that tells me I need to get back into shape.

## Where Do Our Rules Come From?

Similar to our beliefs and values, our personal rules are instilled in us from an early age. However, we do develop new rules as we go through significant stages of our lives, such as when we start school, university, and get a job. We generally model our rules from other people in our lives through observation and experience. The challenge for a lot of people, however, is that the rules they created at these different times in their lives never change. They become fixed. Robbins challenges us to change these old rules by pondering the following questions:

- Are the rules that guide your life today still appropriate for who you've become?
- Have you clung to rules that helped you in the past, but hurt you in the present?
- Have you clung to any inappropriate rules from your childhood/adolescence?

Life is changing all the time! It truly is a variable event. Therefore, if our rules are fixed and not appropriately flexible (like those highlighted by Ellis), they are going to cause us unnecessary pain.

By now you may be starting to recognise a few of the rules you live by. One sure-fire method of identifying if you have a rule about something is noticing when a situation causes you frustration or anger. Take a step back and ask yourself, 'Why am I upset about that? What rule might I have about this?'

In some cases, you may have a perfectly valid response, but in most circumstances, it's probably an unresourceful personal rule triggering your reaction. This is a great opportunity to develop your ego strength and strive for flexibility.

## Achieving Balance

By now you may be starting to recognise a few of the rules you live by. So, how can we get the most out of our rules, and how do you discern which rules are right for you? Figure 4-1 below provides a guideline for how to categorise your rules and respondent behaviour.

There are some rules or personal standards that you will never bend on; these belong in the top right-hand corner (R2). The other category of rules that fit in this corner is those rules that you must adhere to for personal change to occur. When we changed Sarah's values hierarchy, we had to introduce new rules so she could consciously make the right decisions around her new value of health. Some of these included:

- You must take the stairs over an elevator when there is an option.
- You must drink six glasses of water throughout the day.
- You must eat a piece of fruit before a biscuit or some other sugary food.

If you want to change anything in your life, first you must change your value system. Then you must raise your standards by putting Must Rules in place to support that change.

Figure 4-1

**Balancing Your Must Rules and Should Rules**

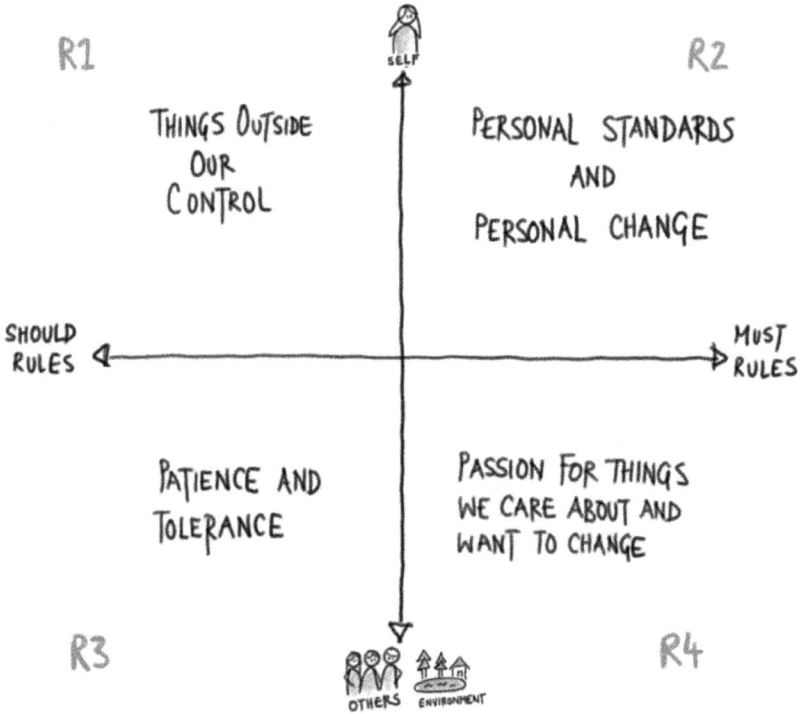

We should examine any Must Rules we have around things that are outside of our control (R1), such as, 'I can't go for my run if it's raining' or 'People must always be polite.' Pay attention to your thoughts and emotions, they will help you uncover these rules.

Then, consciously change these Must Rules to Should Rules (or no rules at all!) If I've got a rule about public transport that states 'Buses must always be on time, the bus driver must be polite and welcoming, and buses must be clean and comfortable,' I'm going to have a bad day before it even starts! Let go of those things you can't control.

Considering the lower left-hand quadrant (R3), we need to practice patience, tolerance, and understanding. People are going to have different views of the world than we have. This is what makes life interesting and fun. Some people may have Should Rules for things that are Must Rules for us, and conversely, we may have Should Rules for things that are Must Rules for them.

Lastly, the lower right-hand quadrant (R4) represents those things we are passionate about; an example might be environmental causes or animal welfare. What we need to be mindful of is that sometimes overzealous behaviour can lead to the opposite result of what we want.

I always remind my clients who are running into obstacles that are causing them no end of frustration of a phrase I picked up from Michael Nell in his book *Supercoach*: 'Be committed but detached.' Be committed to the outcome, but detached from the specific way you get there, detached from the emotion of—for example—frustration or anger.

Too many Must Rules will drain your enthusiasm for life. Having too many Must Rules increases the chances of them being broken, leading to frustration and upset. (Not only for yourself, but people with a lot of Must Rules drive others crazy, as well!)

Equally, having no standards for yourself will lead to an unfulfilling life. To enjoy life and still make progress in the areas that are important to you, you must have a balance between your Must Rules and your Should Rules.

## What's It Going to Be?

Believe it or not, other people don't cause us to get upset. In fact, every upset you've ever had with another person is not the other person's fault; it's your rules that are causing you to feel upset, angry, or sad.

Consider this: before reading about the personal rules, you may not have been aware of the impact they have on you and others. Therefore, is it possible that, just like another person doesn't know your rules, you may not know theirs? Of course it is! Explaining to the other person why you're upset will help them understand you better. Also, if you want to understand someone's rules about a particular aspect of their life, ask them, "What has to happen in order for you to feel X" or "What was it about that that caused you to feel X?"

If it's our personal rules that cause us upset, and not the other person, then we have a choice. What's it going to be, our rules or the relationship? Remember, our rules are arbitrary, we've made them up! Personal rules should enhance your relationships and the quality of your life, not destroy them. As Robbins suggests, any time we're conflicted between a rule and a relationship, the question we need to ask ourselves is, "What's more important, my relationship or my rules?" Only you can answer this question.

## Rules for Creating Rules

After working with people from all walks of life, I think it's safe to say that the majority of people have loads of rules around how to feel bad about themselves (disempowering rules) and very few around how to feel happy and empowered. As I mentioned earlier, our personal rules are meant to empower our relationships and enhance the quality of our lives, so what are the rules for setting up our rules?

### *Our Rules Must Be Achievable*

Our rules must set us up for success. Having a rule that is not achievable is simply setting us up for failure and misery. For example, if I had a rule about maintaining five percent body fat, I'd be miserable! I would be failing all the time. As much as I'd like to work out and eat well every day, the reality is sometimes I just don't get the time. I have other values that are a higher priority for me, like family and growth. Your rules are about achieving a balance that is right for you.

## The Outcomes Must Be Within Our Control

The outcome of our rules must be within our control. If we can't control the situation, then again, we are setting ourselves up for failure. For example, a rule that would cause me to fail every time would be, 'Everyone must talk to me respectfully and in calm and measured tones.' I can't control how other people communicate.

However, a rule I can create for myself that would be in my control is, 'I must talk to others respectfully and in calm and measured tones.' This I can do.

## Have More Rules That Make You Happy and Successful

If you have rules that are driving behaviour that is leading you to places you don't want to be or causing you unnecessary upset, change them! Eradicate any rule that makes you feel bad, and create rules that make you feel happy.

One rule that everyone should have is, "I must forgive myself for mistakes made in the past." The past is over. Whatever happened then is behind you; it doesn't define who you are or the future you are creating for yourself... unless you keep going back there and reliving it.

Draw a line in the sand, determine your new rules for happiness and success, and take the actions that will bring you everything you deserve in life.

And everyone deserves happiness.

**Realigning Your Rules**

Now, grab your notebook and pen and take a moment to answer these questions:

1. What has to happen for you to feel successful?
2. What has to happen for you to feel loved?
3. What has to happen for you to feel confident?

What are the other areas of your life you should create rules for? Check out your values hierarchy and create empowering rules for your core values.

Now that you've written down your rules for the important areas of your life, quickly review the Rules for Creating Rules. Have you set yourself up for success?

## Coach's Tip

Pay attention to the situations or people that cause you to get upset. Being aware of how events or situations make you feel is a strong indicator that you may have a rule about what just happened. Reflect back on times in the past that caused you to get upset and think about these questions:

- What were your rules about that situation?
- Were they the right rules at the time?
- If someone broke one of your rules, were they aware of them?
- Are those rules still valid for who you are becoming as a person now?
- What new rules can you create to replace them that would lead you to more success and even greater happiness?

Now that you have shattered the chains that were holding you back, created a new direction in your life through your values hierarchy, and developed personal rules to propel you in that direction, it's time to understand why we do the things that we do.

# CHAPTER 5

# The Driving Forces Behind It All

*What would changing your two primary needs lead to?*

In the opening chapter of this book, you may remember me describing an incident where I was inadequately, and some might say unnecessarily, defending myself in a boardroom. This wasn't the first time I embarrassed myself with that kind of behaviour, and it wasn't the last. It took me a while to discover the underlying drivers for the behaviour, but once I did, I was able to make the changes which have helped me become more like the person I want to be.

Underlying every action we take is a driving cause; everything we do is done to meet a psycho-social need. If you've ever studied management, you've no doubt come across Maslow's Hierarchy of Needs (Figure 5-1). I remember sitting in an exam hall drawing the triangle and filling it in from bottom to top to show that I understood this concept. Like everything in life, understanding something is always the first step, but to truly know it we have to apply it to our own lives. Although the management studies have latched onto the

Humanistic Perspective of Psychology (of which Maslow was a pioneer), these teachings go far beyond the nine-to-five and have a huge impact on every decision we make. Understanding Maslow's needs and how they relate to you will help you understand what makes you tick.

Maslow's hierarchy of needs theory provides a theory of human needs and a theory of human motivation to achieve these needs. He created his hierarchy of needs based on the tendency and likelihood of appearance:

1. Physiological needs
2. Safety needs
3. Belongingness or love needs
4. Esteem needs
5. Self-actualisation

These needs were further categorised as deficiency needs (physiology, safety, belongingness and love) and growth needs (esteem and self-actualisation). Maslow's theory proposed that when an individual is unsatisfied, they are motivated to dominate the next need in the hierarchy. Upon dominating this need, the gratification achieved subsides, further motivating the individual to dominate the next higher need. This cycle continues until all needs on the hierarchy have been met, and the individual achieves self-actualisation.

First off, it's important to recognise that Maslow got it half right. He did accurately identify the human needs that are in each of us. However, they are not hierarchical; they are in fact competing needs which we often, at an unconscious level, trade off against one another as we go about our daily lives.

In her book *Relationship Breakthrough*, Chloé Madanes recognises the importance of Maslow's Hierarchy of Needs and combines these insights with those of John A. Schindler. Schindler, in *How to Live 365 Days a Year*, proposed that there are six basic needs that all human beings strive for: Love, Security, Creative Expression,

Figure 5-1

**Maslow's Hierarchy of Needs Model**

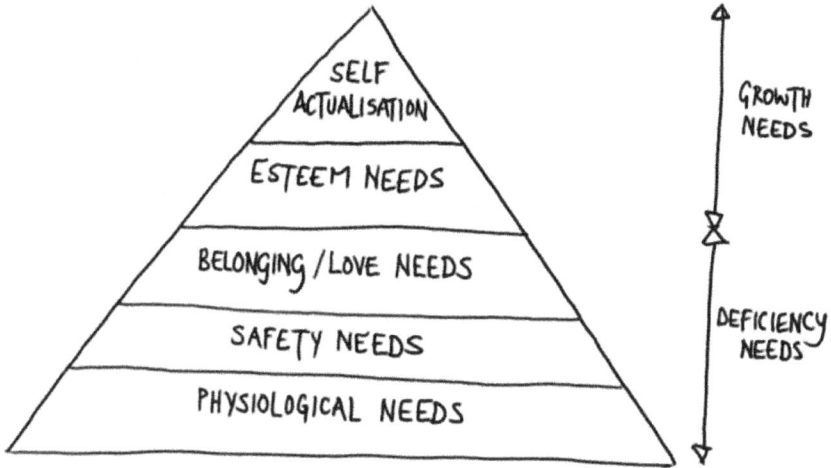

Recognition, New Experiences, and Self-Esteem.

Changing the language somewhat, Madanes presents a different version of the six basic needs (Figure 5-2).

1. Certainty/Comfort
2. Uncertainty/Variety
3. Significance
4. Love/Connection
5. Growth
6. Contribution

Figure 5-2

**Six Basic Needs Model**

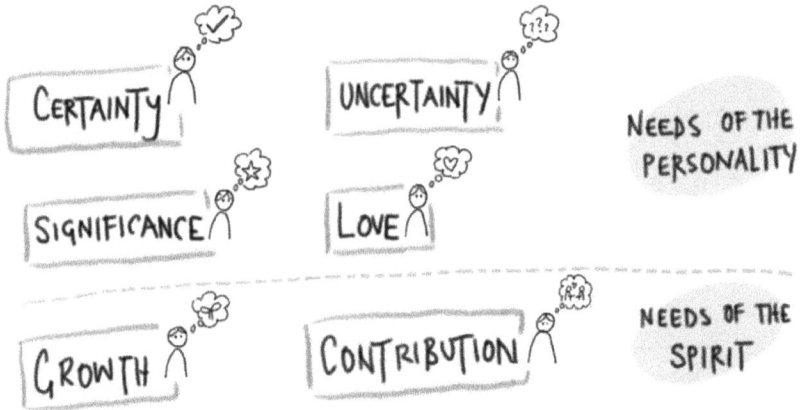

It is through this model that I started to understand what was driving my behaviour. Let's explore this model in a little more detail. Madanes refers to the first four needs (Certainty, Uncertainty, Significance, Love) as Needs of the Personality. No matter who you are or what country you live in, we all must meet these needs on some level. How we meet these needs plays a huge role in who we become as a person and how we live our lives.

The last two needs (Growth and Contribution) are called the Needs of the Spirit. Although these needs are necessary for our happiness and fulfilment, not everyone is successful in finding ways to satisfy these needs. Let's take a closer look at these needs and how they might be driving your behaviour.

*What a man can be, he must be. This need we call self-actualization.*
~ Abraham Maslow

## Needs of the Personality

### *Certainty/Comfort*

Certainty (security, predictability) includes the needs for physical safety and psychological comfort. Everybody wants stability when it comes to their basic necessities: food, shelter or other material resources. Certainty needs are important for survival, for example, the desire for steady employment, health insurance, safe neighbourhoods, and shelter from the elements. I'm sure you've seen those survival shows on television—the first thing the contestants do is seek out shelter and a food source.

Often when people cannot control their physical circumstances, they seek a sense of Certainty through a state of mind, such as religious faith or a positive outlook. A year after the devastating Christchurch earthquakes in February 2011, a news report indicated that church attendance had decreased in every major city in New Zealand except one.

You guessed it: Christchurch.

It's the desire to meet this need that causes people such stress and fear during times of change. People with a high need for Certainty in their lives struggle with change and are reluctant to go too far out of their comfort zone. As a leader, it is important to provide your people with the level of Certainty they need by reinforcing the good job they are doing (find something they're doing right and build on that).

If any of your staff are struggling, it is possible they are experiencing a level of trepidation about their future with the organisation. And if their need for Certainty isn't being met by you, they will source it somewhere else—for example, with disgruntled colleagues. Talking with disgruntled colleagues will definitely meet their need for Certainty, because it's a safe place to rant and they know they'll be supported.

The level of Certainty people need varies from person to person. Living in a single room drawing unemployment benefits might be enough for one person, whereas another might need to have their mortgage paid off and be making a million dollars a year to feel a proper level of Certainty. Although Certainty is necessary for us all, what makes up this need varies from individual to individual.

## Uncertainty/Variety

The contrasting need of Certainty is Uncertainty or Variety (surprise, conflict chaos, change, instability). We all have the need to be challenged, to exercise our body and emotions. Some people may seek Uncertainty through a number of ways: stimuli, change of scene, physical activity, mood swings, entertainment, food, etc. How boring would your life be if you were certain about everything you did? This was the basic premise of Michael Douglas's character in the movie *The Game*.

We need Uncertainty in our lives to challenge us, to help us grow our comfort zone. People with a high need for Uncertainty in their lives are always looking for the next big challenge. During a restructure, they are looking for the opportunities. 'It's about time!' they say, and 'Bring it on!' They're not content living a life where everything is mapped out.

Many people with this mindset are entrepreneurs or adventurers and shake up their lives in different ways to meet this need. If you've got someone like this on your team and they are signalling to you they are getting bored and need a challenge, it's wise to listen. It that need isn't being met by you, they will seek it somewhere else... potentially with a new company. Your organisation might be a terrific place to work, the pay might be great, and the team might be really close. but sometimes that's not enough for those seeking variety. They need to be stimulated and challenged.

Just as a level of Certainty is important for us to function day in and day out, it's the excitement that comes from new challenges in life that makes us feel alive, that we're growing. As with Certainty, people meet their need for Uncertainty in different ways. Watching the news or eating at a new restaurant might be enough for some, whereas others seek out a different kind of variety like extreme sports or taking on short-term work contracts at different organisations.

Certainty and Uncertainty work in balance with each other. Even those with a high need for Certainty need some kind of Uncertainty for stimulation, while living in a state of Uncertainty all the time can be pretty exhausting.

## Significance

The next need we have is the need for Significance, the need to feel important. The need for Significance starts out when we are very young and all want to be seen as special. Children often compete with one another to stand out and gain their parent's affection and praise. It's not uncommon for people to constantly compare themselves with others in order to feel superior in some way.

There are generally three ways people meet this need for Significance. The first is making themselves feel important by belittling someone else's achievement or berating them in public. Others meet this need by being the loudest, the funniest or the most inappropriate. When an individual is feeling insignificant, the quickest way to achieve Significance is to lose their temper, to shout and become aggressive. Immediately the attention is on them (and only them!), and they achieve a sense of importance in that moment. Although this is a dysfunctional approach, the person unconsciously achieves their goal.

If you're thinking this is what drove some of my behaviours during that board meeting, you're spot on!

The second way of achieving Significance is by putting yourself out there in a positive way: by achieving great things, giving your energy for the benefit of another, becoming a role model or overcoming a seemingly insurmountable challenge.

Lastly, many people meet their need for Significance in neutral ways. People who want to stand out from the crowd might get tattoos and piercings in unusual places. They'll dress a little differently or have out-of-the-norm hair colouring or styles.

It's key to remember that individuals can also meet their need for Significance by talking about problems they seem to derive more pleasure complaining about than overcoming. Anytime someone does something to draw attention to themselves deliberately, they are possibly feeling a need to be recognised.

As a leader, it is easy to meet this need in others simply by praising, as Dale Carnegie recommends, heartily and often. Of course, praise has to be honest and specific, and it's important to always look for the positive even in a seemingly negative situation.

## *Love/Connection*

As with all the needs, the need for Love or Connection (warmth, tenderness, desire) varies from individual to individual, but everyone has a need for connecting with others in their lives. Some people need others around them all the time; they are involved in lots of different groups and events and have a high disposition towards social engagements. At the other end of the spectrum are those who are happy to be mostly on their own. Every now and again they'll mingle or be part of a club, but their need is far below that of the social butterfly.

Some people rarely experience Love, but meet their need through other relationships, whether through work or the community.

You may remember the important role the desire for love and acceptance plays in the formation of the personality. That need is a major driver in our lives.

Even though some people might push others away and seem like they do not want to be close to anyone, this is often a basic defence mechanism to protect them from getting hurt. These people are often driven by fear.

# Needs of the Spirit

## Growth

Growth is a necessary part of life; if we're not growing, we're dying. Growth is also synonymous with change. Everything changes in life. We grow from infants to children, from adults to old age. Because Growth is synonymous with change, it contrasts with Certainty.

Growth can be achieved in any aspect of our lives, spiritually, physically, or academically. One of the best ways to Grow is to try something new and gain the experience firsthand.

Another way we meet the need for Growth is through the surprises life brings us. Life is a variable event, and it comes with different challenges. Some people have experienced tremendous growth through trauma or life-changing experiences like moving to a new country or having a baby. These experiences have stretched them, challenged them, and forced them to dig deeper to overcome the situation.

## Contribution

Many people believe that Growth is driven by the desire to contribute. There is no greater act of kindness than going beyond our needs to help others. Everyone can contribute in some way, such as donating time to a charity, mentoring a child, planting trees, or getting involved in a community project.

Meeting the need for Contribution is one of the fastest ways to achieve happiness and fulfilment. Madanes even goes so far as to state, "A life is incomplete without the sense that one is making a contribution to others or to a cause."

## Primary Driving Forces

Of the six needs, we each have two that dominate our decision-making more than the others. These needs are felt so deeply, they are key driving forces for our lives.

Needs can be met in healthy and unhealthy ways. For example, take the need of Certainty. One person might meet this need by controlling their environment and everyone in it. Another person might meet this need by pushing others away and not trusting anyone.

If a person's need is not being met, it will lead to stress. Often, if this is a primary need, the person will focus on the single need to the exclusion of all others, and those needs will begin to suffer as well.

Table 5-1 provides some examples of how we can meet our needs in resourceful or unresourceful ways.

**Identifying Your Needs**
Grab your notebook and pen. List your needs in order of importance to you (1 – 6).

Now identify your two primary needs. How do they influence the direction of your life?

Table 5-1

**Meeting Our Needs**

| Need | Resourceful | Unresourceful |
|------|-------------|---------------|
| Certainty/Comfort | Paying off your mortgage or achieving a college degree | Controlling one's environment and even other people |
| Uncertainty/Variety | Meeting new people, actively trying new things | Having an extra-marital affair, taking risks that might harm others |
| Significance | Working hard to be the best at something, giving your time to a worthy cause | Going on about a problem without taking action to resolve it, being loud and obnoxious |
| Love/Connection | Being kind, developing close relationships | Forcing someone to express their appreciation for you out of fear |
| Growth | Becoming a better person | Becoming a selfish person who harms others |
| Contribution | Giving of yourself to a good cause, helping a person in need | Contributing to a cause that causes harm to others or the environment |

In my earlier years, I was primarily driven by the needs of Significance and Certainty. But how I was meeting those needs wasn't making me happy, because I sought to meet them through my external environment. I relied on other people giving me compliments to feel significant or to provide me with direction. Eventually, I recognised this was holding me back in life.

The great thing about our needs is they, like our beliefs and values, are instilled in us at an early age. That means we can change

Figure 5-3

**Changing My Primary Needs**

OLD NEEDS

SIGNIFICANCE

CERTAINTY

NEW NEEDS

GROWTH

CONTRIBUTION

them if how we are meeting them is not fulfilling for us. This is exactly what I did. I examined all the needs in detail, then looked at my values and asked myself, 'Who do I want to be?' Recognising that my primary needs weren't supporting me, I decided to change them to needs that would empower me. I also had to reassess how I would meet my old primary needs (Significance and Certainty). Figure 5-3 illustrates this transition.

Although on the surface, changing the priority of these needs might look superficial, I found that as I focused on what these needs meant to me and how I would go about meeting them, substantial changes started to occur in my life. By turning my attention to Growth, I looked at the challenges life threw at me as opportunities to grow and stretch myself. In fact, I started to seek these out. I returned to my studies and started my coaching business. I was terrified giving up a steady job with a stable income in a profession I was well-versed in (Certainty). As mentioned earlier, I see Growth and Uncertainty closely linked, and I knew if I wanted to move forward, I would have to change the way I met my need for Certainty.

To move forward, I had to start meeting my needs for Significance and Certainty internally instead of externally. I created a belief that, no matter what life throws at me, I can deal with it. I may not know how I'll do it, but I'll find a way. Couple this with my new primary need for Growth, and I would always be looking for new things to learn. This turned out to be a useful combination when I was starting my own coaching business!

Addressing my needs for Significance internally created a deeper sense of confidence. I don't need to be perfect, I'm always learning. Therefore, for me, there is no such thing as failure; there is only learning that contributes to my Growth.

I Contribute to the lives of hundreds of people every year through my coaching and by supporting my children in being kind, happy, and courageous.

You can't help but meet the need of Uncertainty or Variety when you're running your own business, and on top of that, with the range of clients I work with, I never know what challenges they'll bring to the table.

I'm fortunate to be able to meet my need for Love through my family and by connecting on a deep level with my clients.

Therefore, by the simple act of changing my two primary needs, everything has changed for me. What would changing your two primary needs lead to?

Let's revisit my boardroom experience. With my new primary needs in place, how would I have acted differently? I imagine I would have sought a connection with the Chief Financial Officer by asking questions to try and understand where he was coming from. As Stephen Covey advises in his bestselling book, *The 7 Habits of Successful People*, seek first to understand, and then to be understood.

**Your New Primary Needs**

Review your notes from the previous exercise. If your primary needs don't support you in the direction you want to take in life, identify the two needs that will.

Write these in your notebook. Next write down how you will meet these needs. What do you have to change about your old primary needs so you can continue to move forward?

I know this approach works, because I have employed it to great effect several times since.

## Coach's Tip

Take a moment to review your coat of arms, empowering beliefs, values, and rules. Make any changes that are necessary to ensure they are all aligned with your basic needs and how you are meeting them.

If you're interested in improving your relationships, pick someone who is important to you and, against each of the basic needs, ask yourself this question: "On a scale of 1 to 10, how am I meeting this person's need?" What would you have to do to achieve a ten in every area?

PART TWO

# Bouncing Back

*Resilience is, of course, necessary for a warrior. But a lack of empathy isn't.*

*~ Phil Klay*

# The Wise Old King

The old king sat on his throne surrounded by his advisers, staring intently at two landscape paintings presented before him. The two paintings were the finalists of a competition the king was holding, and all the artists across the land had been invited to participate.

The theme of the competition was 'peace, calm, and tranquillity'. The painting on the left was of a beautiful lake. An early morning mist rose gently from the still waters surrounded by tall fir trees, reaching into a clear blue sky.

The picture on the right was, in contrast, of a raging waterfall. Gallons of water surged over jagged grey rocks; the surrounding trees were bent over from stormy winds, and a deluge of rain lashed the landscape, pouring down from angry dark clouds.

To all the advisers looking on, the winner was clear… obviously the painting on the left more than met the winning criteria. They wondered what was taking the king so long, but none of them rushed him, or even questioned him. They all bore great respect for the king, and what he had achieved during his reign.

After some time, the old king raised his hand, pointing to the landscape painting to his right. "This," he said, "is the winner. This painting represents true peace and tranquility to me."

*The court advisors were stunned. They didn't know what to say or where to look. Had the old man finally lost his marbles?*

*Aware of their confusion, the king reached forward and placed his finger between painted jagged rocks on the cliff face.*

*"The ability to remain calm and centered when all around you is chaos truly is a gift. This represents true peace and tranquility."*

*He removed his finger, and the court advisors leaned in to see, on a tiny ledge, a small bird calmly sitting on her nest as the storm raged around her.*

CHAPTER 6

# The Psychology of Stress

*If we fail to adapt to our stressors, we enter into the third and final stage of the GAS model.*

I woke to the sound of my wife screaming. I was lying on the floor of a serviced apartment at four a.m. in New Plymouth, slumped against the vanity cabinet in the small bathroom. I felt the adrenaline surge through my veins as my wife pulled me into more of a seated position, and blinked my eyes back into focus.

What I saw next made me realize it was time to change. My daughter stood peering through the bathroom door, woken by the screams and staring in confusion and fear at me—her father—crumpled on the floor.

It took me a while to work up the strength, but eventually I made it back to the bed.

How did it all go so terribly wrong? Roll back the clock to four months earlier, and you would have found me working a minimum of sixty hours a week, studying a psychology paper (I was considering taking on two!), trying to give as much time to my family as I could, and trying to stay in shape. (The waistband of my trousers was having a few challenges of its own!)

This is what my daily routine looked like. I would rise early to work from home, go into work, work through the day, wolf down my lunch at my desk, race home in the evening to spend time with my girls, and spend the rest of the evening studying after they went to bed.

And, yes! I have a very supportive… and patient… wife!

I was really looking forward to the break over Christmas and planned to leave all my work and study behind me, so I could just enjoy the couple of weeks with my family.

But for the last four months, I'd been living on adrenaline. And although I was keeping a close eye on how I was feeling, I wasn't taking those little breaks to release the building allostatic load (more on this later). My immune system was battling just to keep me standing, and it eventually exhausted itself, leaving me exposed to "a cocktail of viruses" as the doctor referred to it.

This was my first experience of burnout. I've been tired before, and I've worked really hard before, but never had I exhausted myself to the point where my body forced me to stop.

Burnout is the result of extreme stress over a prolonged period of time. This is just one of the results stress can have on us—so what is stress? How does it impact us physically, mentally, emotionally? And lastly, how can we make it our friend?

## The Importance of the Stress Response

In the days when we were running around in animal skins, everything was trying to kill us. Animals, floods, too much heat, too much cold, disease, hunger, avalanches, other 'people'… everything! The stress response had a very specific purpose: to keep us alive! So, if, for example, we came across a sabre-toothed tiger, the sympathetic nervous system would kick in, causing the fight-or-flight response. Our adrenal glands would flood our system with a whole heap of stress-related hormones like norepinephrine, adrenaline, and cortisol. Norepinephrine and adrenaline give us an immediate boost of energy and strength to help us overcome the immediate threat.

This whole process happens automatically and occurs through the autonomic nervous system (Figure 6-1). This system has two parts: the sympathetic nervous system, which triggers the immediate mobilisation of the body's resources for a survival situation, and the parasympathetic nervous system, which returns the body to homeostasis (a balanced state.)

## The Causes of Stress

Before we go any further into stress and the impact it has on the body, take a moment to answer this question: "What causes you stress?"

---

**What Causes You Stress?**
Take out your notebook and quickly jot down the things that cause you stress on a daily basis.

---

Whenever I ask this question in my seminars and workshops, I get a range of answers that encompasses the following:

- Money
- Children
- Not having enough time
- Too much to do
- Work colleagues

Figure 6-1

**The Autonomic Nervous System**

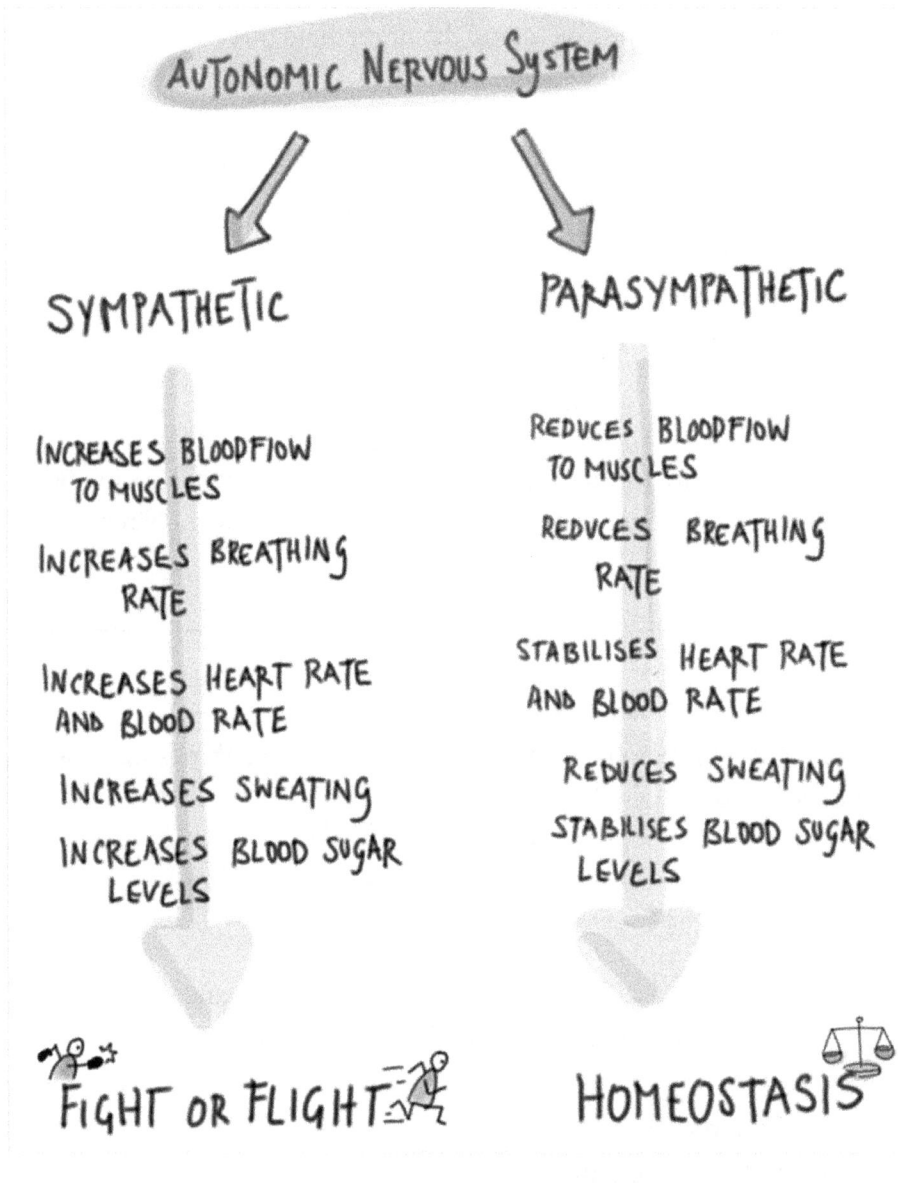

AUTONOMIC NERVOUS System

SYMPATHETIC

INCREASES BLOODFLOW TO MUSCLES

INCREASES BREATHING RATE

INCREASES HEART RATE AND BLOOD RATE

INCREASES SWEATING

INCREASES BLOOD SUGAR LEVELS

FIGHT OR FLIGHT

PARASYMPATHETIC

REDUCES BLOODFLOW TO MUSCLES

REDUCES BREATHING RATE

STABILISES HEART RATE AND BLOOD RATE

REDUCES SWEATING

STABILISES BLOOD SUGAR LEVELS

HOMEOSTASIS

- Not fitting comfortably into my clothes
- Having an injury
- School pick-ups and drop-offs
- Being shouted at
- Being late
- No direction at work
- Incompetent bosses
- Being sick
- Demands from other people
- Automated phone answering services
- Too many emails
- Traffic
- Inconsiderate drivers

I'm sure you can add to this list quite easily. Now that we have this list in place, I'd like you to imagine this scenario…

You and I are out on a boat, fishing in the harbour. We're not too far out, maybe five hundred metres or so. We're not wearing life jackets, and we're having a great time laughing and joking when out of nowhere a freak wave appears and topples the boat.

We both go flying into the water and, almost at the same time, we reach the surface. Now, you're a confident swimmer, and you come up laughing and joking. "Where did that wave come from?" you ask between fits of laughter.

Me, on the other hand, I'm not that confident in the water. In fact, I can't swim at all, so I'm scrambling to get any kind of grip on the side of the boat. I'm holding on for dear life, and you say to me, "Don't worry. Stay with the boat, I'll swim in and get help."

So off you go, giggling to yourself about the look of panic on my face. You're thinking to yourself how funny this will be when we're down at the pub later on.

Meanwhile, I'm still holding onto the boat, white-knuckled. I start to realise just how cold the water actually is. I'm trying to remember how long it takes for somebody to get hypothermia, and my body starts to shiver uncontrollably. I notice that the tide is taking the boat further out to sea, and I'm thinking that once a current gets hold of it, I'm a goner!

Suddenly, I see a shadow in the water and my heart leaps! Was it a shark? Sharks are common in these waters—what else could it be!

I try and grab a handhold higher on the surface of the upturned boat and kick my legs in desperation. My breathing becomes short, and I can feel my heart pounding in my chest. My mind screams, "I don't want to die!"

It's quite clear from this scenario that my body has triggered the sympathetic nervous system and I'm experiencing the fight-or-flight response. But let's take a closer look at this scenario. What's the difference between you and me? We're both experiencing the same event at exactly the same time, in exactly the same circumstances. Why am I freaking out and under immense stress and you're not?

## The Perils of Stress

Extensive research has been carried out to determine what causes stress. Linda Brannon and Jess Feist in their book, *Health Psychology*, state "Neither the environmental event nor the person's response defines stress; rather, the individual's perception of the psychological situation is the critical factor. This perception includes potential harm, threats, and challenges as well as the individual's perceived ability to cope with them." Therefore, stress can be revised down to a simple formula (Figure 6-2). It's not the event that causes us stress; it's the meaning we put on the event.

Let's put this into the context of our scenario. I'm freaking out, and you're not. What do you have in this situation that I don't have?

Figure 6-2

---

**The Stress Formula**

$$STRESS = RELATIONSHIP\,(\,YOU + ENVIRONMENT\,)$$

---

The answer is you have a particular skill that can be applied immediately: you can swim, and I can't. You don't need to be stressed in this situation. Your interpretation is: we've fallen into the water, so I'll just tread water here and get my bearings. If anything, you might be experiencing a positive stress called eustress (we'll cover this in the next chapter).

On the other hand, my interpretation of the situation is that we've fallen into the water and I'm going to drown.

What else in this scenario are you doing differently than me? You're thinking to yourself that this is hilarious! You can't wait to share the joke with everyone at the pub later that evening. You're envisioning a positive outcome.

Me? Well, I'm imagining I'm going to get hyperthermia and get eaten by sharks! I'm assigning a completely different meaning to the situation, one that calls for my body to respond with the highest alert because I'm going to die! At least in my mind anyway.

Whether the body is experiencing an actual threat or a perceived threat, it responds in exactly the same way. Stress is most likely to be aroused when we're feeling vulnerable in a situation, the situation is of personal importance to us, and we lack the resources to deal with it. Of course, 'importance' is determined by our perception and evaluation (Figure 6-3).

Figure 6-3

**Evaluating a Situation: The Unconscious Process**

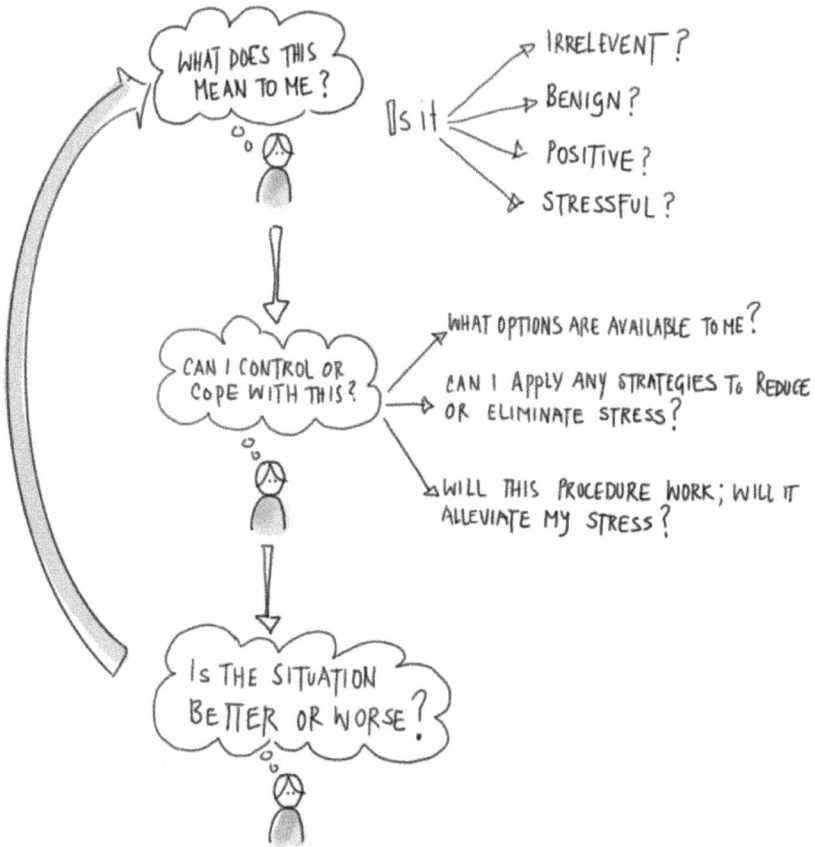

When we evaluate a situation, we do it automatically and at an unconscious level.

The first thing we ask ourselves is: 'What does this mean to me?' If there are no negative consequences, this is the end of the process.

However, if we perceive the situation as stressful, then we ask: 'Can I control or cope with this?' Two things kick into play here. If we have the skills to deal with the situation, the stress response disappears.

However, even if we don't have the skills to deal with a particular situation, we can still employ mental strategies to remain calm and prevent the fight-or flight-response (we'll talk about how to do this in the next chapter).

Lastly, we check: 'Is the situation better or worse?' This can either lead us to spiral down or spiral up and out.

These evaluative questions loop, and we continue to assess the situation until the perceived threat has passed.

---

**Reevaluating What Causes You Stress**
Review the list of items you wrote earlier and jot down what this means to you against each of them.

Now list the skills you might need to develop so stress doesn't become an issue for you anymore.

Lastly, if there are no specific skills you need to learn (for example, being stuck in traffic), what new meaning can you put on the event so that isn't stressful for you?

---

## The Silent Killer

The stress response evolved with one purpose in mind, to enable us to survive. We're here because our ancestors were really good at evaluating threatening situations. It's important to recognise that the purpose of the stress response is to help us through temporary events that we perceive are a threat to us. It works really well in these situations, but does not work so well over prolonged periods without a break. Here's why.

Earlier, we mentioned the hormones that are released by the sympathetic nervous system, and how norepinephrine and adrenaline give us a surge of energy and prepare us for fight or flight. Now we will discuss cortisol, and what its role is.

The purpose of cortisol is to regulate blood pressure and maintain fluid balance during the stressful period. In a normal stress-induced situation, the body will naturally absorb these hormones through physical activity, such as running away or fighting. This is healthy and in line with what nature intended. However, if we're not exerting ourselves through physical activity, the stress hormones take a while to be absorbed back into the system.

The constant presence of cortisol in our system suppresses the immune system and can lead to all sorts of ailments, including ulcers, colds, flu, skin complaints, headaches and migraines, fatigue and back pain. Cortisol also inhibits the body's ability to break down harmful fats, which end up being deposited along the walls of the coronary arteries. Over time, this build-up of plaque narrows the arteries to the heart, blood flow to the heart is reduced, and the likely result is an eventual myocardial infarction, or heart attack. Figure 6-4 is an illustration of the General Adaptation Syndrome (GAS).

In their book, *Understanding Psychology*, Charles Morris and Albert Maisto describe Hans Seyle as a pioneer in the research of stress. It was he who developed the GAS model for how the body prepares itself for stressful situations. This syndrome is divided into three stages: Alarm, Resistance and Exhaustion.

During the alarm stage, the body mobilises its defences and activates the sympathetic nervous system. However, as mentioned earlier, this is a short-term response and, although useful for emergency situations, the stressful conditions that we may find ourselves in can be prolonged and may not provide us with the opportunity for physical activity, as in the flight response.

During the resistance stage, the body adapts to the stressor and outwardly appears normal. But physiologically, the continuing stress causes ongoing neurological and hormonal changes, leading to what Seyle described as *diseases of adaptation*.

Figure 6-4

---

**The General Adaption Syndrome**

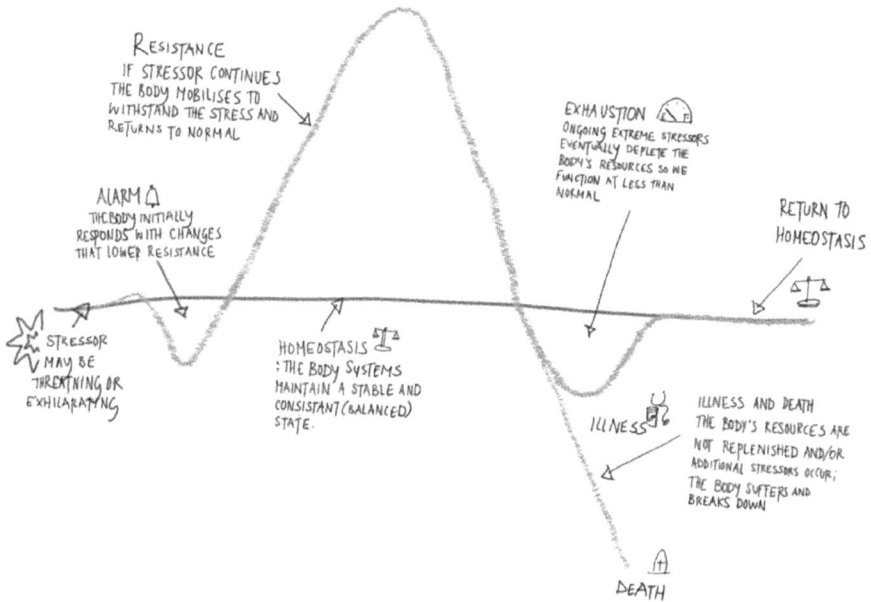

RESISTANCE
IF STRESSOR CONTINUES
THE BODY MOBILISES TO
WITHSTAND THE STRESS AND
RETURNS TO NORMAL

EXHAUSTION
ONGOING EXTREME STRESSORS
EVENTUALLY DEPLETE THE
BODY'S RESOURCES SO WE
FUNCTION AT LESS THAN
NORMAL

RETURN TO
HOMEOSTASIS

ALARM
THE BODY INITIALLY
RESPONDS WITH CHANGES
THAT LOWER RESISTANCE

STRESSOR
MAY BE
THREATENING OR
EXHILARATYNG

HOMEOSTASIS
: THE BODY SYSTEMS
MAINTAIN A STABLE AND
CONSISTANT (BALANCED)
STATE.

ILLNESS

ILLNESS AND DEATH
THE BODY'S RESOURCES ARE
NOT REPLENISHED AND/OR
ADDITIONAL STRESSORS OCCUR;
THE BODY SUFFERS AND
BREAKS DOWN

DEATH

---

Diseases of adaptation include hypertension, cardiovascular disease, peptic ulcers, and so on. If we fail to adapt to our stressors, we enter into the third and final stage of the GAS model, exhaustion.

During the exhaustion stage, the parasympathetic nervous system, normally tasked with keeping the body in a balanced state, is at a low level. This causes the person to become exhausted, which can result in depression and, in extreme circumstances, death.

## How Stressed are You?

If you want to get an indication of what your stress levels are, take the Holmes-Rahe Life Events Rating Scale (Figure 6-5). It's a very simple test that will give you a single score to indicate your likely stress levels.

Figure 6-5

## The Holmes-Rahe Life Events Scale

| Life event | Units | Life event | Units |
|---|---|---|---|
| Death of a spouse | 100 | Child leaving home | 29 |
| Divorce | 73 | Change in work responsibilities | 29 |
| Marital separation | 65 | Outstanding personal achievement | 28 |
| Imprisonment | 63 | Spouse starts or stops work | 26 |
| Death of a family member | 63 | Beginning or end school | 26 |
| Personal injury or illness | 53 | Change in living conditions | 25 |
| Marriage | 50 | Revision of personal habits | 24 |
| Dismissal from work | 47 | Trouble with boss | 23 |
| Retirement | 45 | Change in working conditions | 20 |
| Marital reconciliation | 45 | Change in schools | 20 |
| Change in health of family member | 44 | Change in residence | 20 |
| Pregnancy | 40 | Change in recreation | 19 |
| Sexual difficulties | 39 | Change in church activities | 19 |
| Gain a new family member | 39 | Change in social activities | 18 |
| Business readjustment | 39 | Minor mortgage or loan | 17 |
| Change in financial state | 38 | Change in sleeping habits | 16 |
| Death of a close friend | 37 | Change in number of family reunions | 15 |
| Change to different line of work | 36 | Change in eating habits | 15 |
| Change in frequency of arguments | 35 | Vacation | 13 |
| Major mortgage | 32 | Christmas | 12 |

| Foreclosure of mortgage or loan | 30 | Minor violation of law | 11 |
| Trouble with in-laws | 29 | **Total Score** | |

For each of the events listed below, circle the score you associate with it. **Note -** Only score the event if it occurred in the last twelve months; outside of this period doesn't count.

Add up all the circled scores to get your stress rating. Based on your score, Table 6-1 will help you determine your risk profile of illness.

Does this mean that if you scored greater than 300 you will get sick? Of course not! It depends on how you interpreted those events, and what they meant to you.

Table 6-1

**The Holmes-Rahe Life Events Scale – Risk of Illness**

| Score | Risk of Illness |
| --- | --- |
| Less than 150 | Slight risk of illness |
| Between 150 and 299 | Moderate risk of illness |
| Greater than 300 | At risk of illness |

## Allostatic Load

Let's do an experiment. Take an old-style kettle, fill it up with water, stick a cork in the top of it, and place it on a hot stove. At first, there will be no noticeable difference at all. Then we might hear the water start to bubble and boil. And then, finally, the kettle will blow its cork.

The same can be true about people.

As you can discern from the Life Events Scale above, anything that requires you to make an adjustment in life can cause stress. Life events such as marriage, death, birthdays, attending university, and changing jobs all raise your levels of stress. They are referred to as *life events*, because the majority of people in western civilisation experience these during their lives.

Another category, called catastrophes, can also lead to a significant amount of stress. Examples of catastrophes include earthquakes, civil war, tsunamis, fires, and so on. However, these examples are usually spread out over our lifetime, or we may never even experience them at all.

But there's a third category, and this category is synonymous with the boiling kettle. It's referred to as daily hassles.

Daily hassles are all those little things that by themselves seem to have no impact on us. But as they build up over time, they can cause us to explode! Examples of daily hassles might be interpersonal conflicts, rush hour traffic, noise, heat, concerns about weight, ill health, too many things to do, losing things... they all add up until we reach our limit.

Mary Kunert, in her book *Pathophysiology*, defines the allostatic load as, "symptomatic of immunosuppression and hyperactivity of the sympathetic nervous system." Just as our bodies get exhausted by doing too much without rest, so too can our brain and the immune system.

If you're a leader of yourself or a leader of others, it's important to understand the common causes of stress in the work environment (Figure 6-6) so you can proactively deal with them, or at least understand what might be driving a teammate's behaviour.

Figure 6-6

**Common Causes of Workplace Stress**

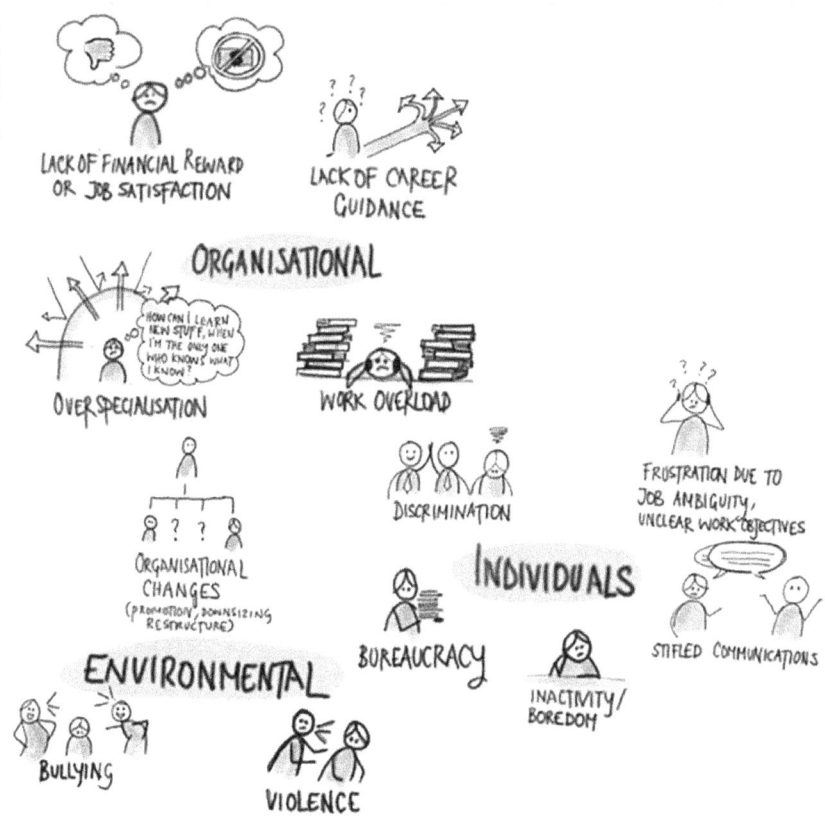

**How Is Your Workplace Stressing You Out?**
Take a look at the common causes of workplace stress and give yourself a mark from 1 – 10 for each of these (10 being the highest).

Now, what are things you can proactively do to reduce these stressors?

Is there a particular meaning you are associating with one of these items?

What new meaning could you create to reduce the stress you feel about this item?

Another tool to help you identify how workplace stress might be impacting you is illustrated in Figure 6-7. Where do you (or your teammates) sit in this diagram?

*The greatest weapon against stress is our ability to choose one thought over another.*
~ William James

## Burning Out

Burnout, in the simplest of terms, is your body's response to chronic stress. It culminates in physical and emotional exhaustion, cynicism and detachment, feelings of ineffectiveness, and lack of accomplishment. As well as understanding the signs of stress within

Figure 6-7

**The Support-Challenge Matrix**

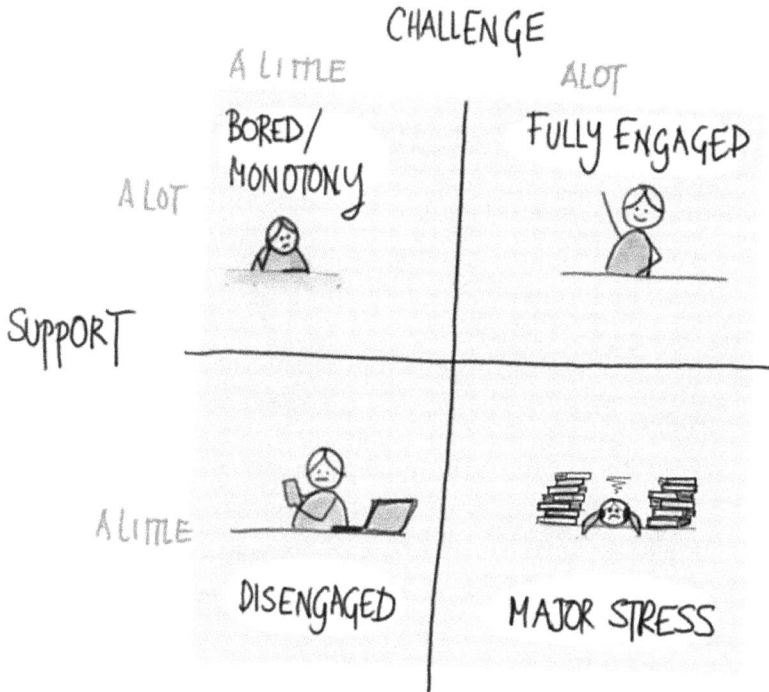

yourself, it's also important to be able to recognise the signs of stress in others before it starts to impact their physical health. So, what are some of the subtle (and not so subtle) signs that you or one of your team might be heading towards burnout? Let's break these down some more...

## *Physical and Emotional Exhaustion*

### Fatigue and insomnia

You may feel anything from being tired and lacking energy for the day to being drained and depleted, dreading the day ahead. Having trouble sleeping is also a sign that things are building, which only exacerbates the fatigue.

### Forgetfulness and Lack of Focus

Not being able to focus and forgetting things is a sign that your cognitive energy is low and your brain is using its resources just to keep you standing.

### Increased Illness

If you're constantly picking up illnesses such as colds and flus, it's a sign that your body is under stress. Its resources, normally more than capable of dealing with whatever comes its way, are being diverted to trying to turn the body back to homeostasis. The immune system is weakened, and the body is vulnerable to attack.

### Anxiety and Anger

Anxiety and anger can be expressed in ways ranging from irritation and tension to angry outbursts. Things that you would normally respond to calmly irritate you, and you react in a less than cordial way.

## *Cynicism and Detachment*

### Loss of Enjoyment

If you lose interest in life and struggle to find the joy in your day, it's probably a good idea to take a step back and take some time out for yourself.

**Pessimism**

We all indulge in negative self-talk every now and then, but when it becomes all-consuming and leads to trust issues with co-workers or family, it is a clear sign that burnout is on the way.

**Isolation and Detachment**

Isolation and detachment from others may be just what the doctor ordered; sometimes some alone time can help us recharge our batteries and bounce back to our normal selves. However, if you find you're isolating and detaching yourself from others because you don't want to be around anyone, this is a sign that your levels of stress have increased to a point where deliberate action is needed. Do what your mind and body are telling you to do… take a break!

### *Signs of Ineffectiveness and Lack of Accomplishment*

**Feeling Apathetic and Hopeless**

If you have the recurring thought, "What's the point?" and it becomes the dominant thought in your mind, this is another sign that things might be getting too much.

**Lack of Productivity and Poor Performance**

Lack of productivity and poor performance, where you were previously knocking the ball out of the park, are a strong indication that enough is enough. Life is too short to get stuck on the treadmill of mediocrity. Take a break and reassess your direction.

It's only when you take time out for yourself, rest, and start doing the things you enjoy will you begin to feel like your normal self again.

So far, we've discussed how we react to stress. We've talked about the possible causes of stress (stressors), and we've looked at what causes stress… we do! Understanding stress and the impacts it has on our psychology and physiology are good to know. However, if we want to go beyond what the average person is capable of, we need to learn to apply a necessary skill for all aspects of life.

# The Impossible Climb

*There once was a bunch of tiny frogs who arranged a climbing competition. The goal of the competition was to reach the top of a very high tower. A big crowd had gathered around the tower to see the race and cheer on the contestants, and the race began...*

*No one in the crowd really believed that the tiny frogs would reach very high. The other frogs in the crowd discussed among themselves.*

*"Oh, WAY too difficult!"*

*"They will NEVER make it to the top..."*

*"Not a chance that they will succeed. The tower is too high!"*

*As the voices in the crowd grew louder, the tiny frogs began collapsing one by one. One group, determined to succeed, climbed higher and higher. The crowd continued to yell, "It is too difficult! No one will make it!"*

*More tiny frogs got tired and gave up.*

*But one frog continued to climb higher and higher and higher. This little frog just wouldn't give up!*

*The crowd couldn't believe it! They were transfixed! This tiny frog, one of them, had achieved the impossible. The cheers and croaks of excitement could be heard for miles around.*

*He must have trained harder than all the other frogs, they mused.*

*He must have had a special diet… dragonflies… they mused.*

*"No," said a tiny frog, "he's my brother, and he didn't train or eat any different from the other frogs."*

*"There must be something different about him," they insisted. "How else could he have achieved such a monumental feat?"*

*"There's no difference," insisted the frog, then she paused. "Oh, wait," she said suddenly. "He's deaf!"*

# CHAPTER 7

# Secrets of Resilience

*When disaster strikes, your sense of permanence will determine how long you give up.*

T he dog was guided to the box, where it stepped onto the metal floor plate. After a moment, the dog yelped in response to an electric shock coming through the floor panel. The shock was no more painful than the shock you might receive from touching a door handle on a dry winter's day, but it was certainly enough to get the dogs attention.

Over time, the dog learned that by pushing a panel with its nose, it could turn off the shock, hence exhibiting control over its environment. This dog belonged to the first group in the experiment.

The second group of dogs had no control over their environment; they were exposed to shocks from which there was no escape.

The last group, the control group, were left alone. No shocks were administered to this group. The following day, the dogs were placed in a shuttle box. The box consisted of two compartments, each with a separate metal floor plate and separated in the middle by an easily jumpable barrier. All three groups of dogs were administered shocks once inside the box.

Those dogs that had previously learned to turn off the shocks with their noses quickly realised they could jump the barrier to escape the shocks. The same was true for the control group. They quickly learned to jump the barrier to escape the pain.

However, the dogs in the second group—the group that initially had no control over its environment—soon gave up and simply lay down on the floor of the box, even though it was being regularly shocked.

Martin Seligman and his colleague, Steven Maier, found that six out of the eight dogs in the 'helpless' group lay down in the box and gave up, while none of the dogs in the group that had learned they could control their environment gave up. Ultimately, they concluded, the dogs gave up because they believed that nothing they did would matter.

Once the experiments were finished, Seligman and Maier led the 'helpless' group of dogs back to the box and trained them to jump over the barrier. When the shocks were applied next time, the dogs leapt the barrier to escape them. They had learned they could control their environment, and they consistently escaped every time the shock was applied.

Some years later, this experiment was repeated by Donald Hiroto; this time not on dogs, but on humans. Rather than using electrical shocks, Hiroto used noise as the offending stimulus.

The results were remarkably similar, leading to the conclusion that human beings can be taught helplessness too. What was really interesting though, is that one in three of Hiroto's volunteers who he tried to make helpless would not give up. Another key finding was that one in ten participants just gave up straight away; they did nothing to escape the noise and just sat there from the beginning. These findings eerily paralleled those of Seligman and Maier, which led to Seligman forming his theory of learned helplessness and explanatory styles.

## Learned Helplessness

Learned helplessness describes the feeling that a person can't escape unpleasant or aversive situations. This impacts motivation and learning, and as you can imagine, is central to depression as well. Seligman observed that some people have an active, coping mindset when faced with disappointment or failure, and others become helpless and depressed. Whether people take action or not comes down to what psychologists call *generalised expectancies*. These expectancies influence a wide range of behaviour.

Seligman proved that, when he and Maier trained the dogs to jump over the barrier in the shuttle box, the dogs learned a new skill and didn't succumb to helplessness when shocked in the future. Therefore, our mindsets can change.

To help us do this, we must understand our explanatory style.

*I will either find a way, or make one.*
~ Hannibal

## Explanatory Styles

Seligman determined that how we make sense of bad events determines if we will become, and remain, depressed.

There are two explanatory styles: optimistic and pessimistic. In Learned Optimism, Seligman outlines the central dimensions of an explanatory style:
1. Permanence – stable, and unlikely to change
2. Pervasiveness – global, or broad, general and widespread
3. Personalisation – internalisation, or self-blame

## *Permanence*

Permanence is about time (permanent versus temporary). People who give up too easily believe that the bad events that happen to them are permanent, and will always be there to affect their lives. When thinking about bad things, they think in terms of absolutes, with words like *always* and *never*. This kind of thinking is synonymous with a permanent, pessimistic style.

On the other hand, people who consistently push through and make the extra effort do so because they believe that bad events are temporary and will pass. They use words like *sometimes* and *recently* when thinking about bad events. People with this mindset have a temporary, optimistic style.

On the flip side, when good things happen, pessimistic thinkers tend to think of those events as temporary and transient in nature. They put it down to luck or people's failings. Optimistic thinkers tend to think the good times will continue to roll, and explain their success by way of their own talent.

When disaster strikes, your sense of permanence will determine how long you give up. Will it be forever, or will it be temporary? The more temporary your thinking, the quicker you'll bounce back from adversity and the more resilient you will become.

## *Pervasiveness*

Pervasiveness is about space (specific versus universal). For example, if you lose your job, do you simply lose confidence about your working abilities, or about your abilities in every aspect of life? Does a downturn in events affect your health, your relationships, and your enjoyment of hobbies?

This way of thinking is known as catastrophising, and causes an event isolated to one area of your life to bleed into every other area. A person who catastrophises, or is of a universal pessimistic mindset, uses universal language to explain their misfortune: *all, everyone,* and *everything.*

At the opposite end of the scale, a person who experiences a negative event, such as losing their job, may suffer a lack of confidence as well, but only in this area. Their explanatory style is specific to that aspect of their lives. Therefore, they are likely to continue with their hobbies and maintain their relationships. They compartmentalise the negative aspect of their life, so it doesn't impact on the other areas. They use specificity in their language too, such as *that, him/her,* and *this.*

How do pessimistic thinkers explain good fortune? You guessed it! They see it as specific to that area of their life. In their mind, it doesn't have any crossover benefit into other areas. The optimist, of course, believes the thing that happened in one area will change everything! It's going to enhance everything they do.

If you can isolate an unfortunate event to the context in which it occurs, you will be able to continue moving forward in the other aspects of your life and maintain a healthy attitude, bouncing back quickly from adversity.

## *Personalisation*

The final dimension of explanatory style is personalisation. Personalisation has to do with where we place blame. Do we blame ourselves (internalise) or blame circumstances (externalise)? How we personalise events or situations has a direct impact on our self-esteem. Those who internalise (blame themselves) tend to beat themselves up more and consequently have low self-esteem. On the other hand, those who externalise (blame external circumstances or others) don't lose self-esteem, and tend to like themselves more.

When a bad event happens, pessimistic thinkers, who internalise, self-reference in the negative. They might say "I'm useless" or "This is all my fault." They take the blame. Optimistic thinkers do the opposite. They naturally look for another explanation of why something went wrong; they rationalise that other people might have been at fault, or it was just bad luck.

Conversely, when good things happen, pessimistic thinkers do the opposite. They look outside themselves for why something went well. But optimists take all the credit! They believe they had a direct influence on making it happen. Because they do this, they like themselves much more, and have a much stronger internal locus of control.

There's no doubt that having an optimistic mindset naturally builds resilience. Now, let's look a little closer at what it means to be an optimist.

Research suggests that people with a pessimistic mindset are more accurate in identifying when they lack control over outcomes. While this can be a useful trait, it also means they see the 'reality' of the situation. They either don't try or they give up too soon. Their belief about what's true becomes a self-fulfilling prophecy for them.

The optimist, however, believes that no matter the challenge, they will find a way. Because of this belief, they don't give up. They keep trying different approaches and strategies, and guess what happens… they find a way! This then becomes a self-fulfilling prophecy. They see things as they want them to be and rally all their resources to make it that way.

People with an optimistic mindset are more successful and more resilient in the face of adversity. It's important to note that optimism and pessimism are on a continuum. Certainly there are people at the extreme ends of the scale, but most of us are in between.

Just because you may default to one way of thinking over another, it's just that: it's a way of thinking… and you can change it. We should look at optimism and pessimism as a tool rather than a personality trait, because both are useful.

Here's a rule of thumb I share with my clients: When the consequences of an action are low, choose to be optimistic about the outcome and go for it 100 percent. However, if the consequences are dire, then it would be prudent to think a little more pessimistically. How should you be thinking in the following scenarios?

Table 7-1

**Should you choose to be optimistic or pessimistic about the situation?**

| Situation | Mindset |
|---|---|
| I've always wanted to do a marathon, but the most I've ever run before is 10 km. Should I do it? | _____ |
| I'm late for a meeting and I'm currently driving 120 km over the speed limit on a tricky section of road. | _____ |
| I failed to get the promotion I wanted in the past, but a new opportunity has opened up. Should I go for it? | _____ |
| I have an important presentation that I need to give tomorrow and know I haven't prepared enough. Should I just wing it? | _____ |
| I know I've had a couple of drinks, but I don't want to face the hassle of getting a taxi home when I could drive. | _____ |

Before we delve into the strategies you can use to develop more optimism, and therefore greater resilience, let's explore the different personality types for an insight into the character traits of the personality that is naturally more resilient than the others.

## Personality Types

Cervone and Pervin, in *Personality, Theory and Research*, define personality as "the psychological qualities that contribute to an individual's enduring and distinctive patterns of feeling, thinking, and behaving." Many people have heard of the Type A personality and the Type B personality, but few have heard of the Type C personality. Let's have a closer look at the traits involved in these and see if you can recognise any in yourself.

## Type A Personality

The Type A personality is probably the most well-researched of all the personalities. It is easily identifiable through traits such as time urgency, impatience, competitiveness, ambition, a hard-driving approach to life, and hostility. Hostility (specifically, defensiveness—suppressed hostility) has been linked with the narrowing of the arteries leading to the heart and the early onset of heart disease.

Type A are poor delegators, but may do so with reluctance, trepidation, and impatience. Type As seldom have time to appreciate those around them and are quick to criticize. They are low in empathy and find it difficult to express affection. What drives the Type A is low self-esteem and a burning desire to gain the approval of others through an unending series of achievements.

## Type B Personality

The Type B personality is much more relaxed about life. In contrast to Type A, they are less 'time urgent' and are much more gracious around people. They delegate better and are open to the opinions of others. They easily overlook the small mistakes others might make and are much less critical. Their family life has noticeably less tension and they naturally express affection and empathy.

Type B personalities have a healthy self-esteem and don't feel the need to seek validation from others through achievements. Because of their ability to give affection freely, they also receive this in abundance from others, further validating them as worthwhile individuals.

## *Type C Personality*

In the previous chapter, we discussed how stressful events can lead to illness. In 1984, this piqued the interest of psychologists Maddi and Kobasa. They studied individuals who thrived under conditions of constant and stressful life-impacting events, and identified traits they referred to as hardiness. These traits align closely with those of the Type C personality.

The Type C personality is a combination of the strengths of both the A Type and the B Type personalities, with a few additional traits thrown in, creating a potent cocktail for facing any challenge with vitality and success.

In short, the Type C personality is a performance model for us all... and it can be learned. Type Cs are optimistic and confident. They enjoy the things they do, they are spontaneous when making decisions, are focused on the task at hand, and full of energy and vitality. They experience stressful events as important and interesting, as things they can influence and as opportunities for growth.

The specific traits aligned to hardiness are:

- Challenge
- Commitment
- Control

### Challenge

Those people who are at the higher end of the challenge curve recognise that change is inevitable, and they are comfortable when it occurs. They see it as a natural process, an opportunity to flex their creative muscles. They rise to the challenge of any adversity and difficulty, and tend to thrive in this environment, often turning hardship into opportunity.

A lot of the time, especially in our 'you can have it instantly' society, we give up to easily. Any time things get a little tough, we convince ourselves this isn't for us. But the truth is, anything worth

Figure 7-1

---

**The 3 Cs of Hardiness**

---

achieving is going to take effort; it's going to take you out of your comfort zone and stretch you. If it was easy, then everyone would be doing it.

Consider the swimmer Michael Phelps. Phelps has achieved the pinnacle of sporting success. He has won more Olympic gold medals than anyone else in history. His swimming stroke is flawless, and quite clearly he's a natural, a genius at what he does. When we look at someone like Phelps, too often we just see his talent and we forget what it took for him to get there. We forget that he trained for more than five hours every day to achieve his success!

In her bestseller, *Grit,* Angela Duckworth reminds us that achievement doesn't come down to talent alone. Duckworth, through her research, proved that effort is the deciding factor. It's effort that separates the great from the mediocre. Her formula reflects this:

Figure 7-2

**Effort Counts Twice**

$$\text{TALENT} \times \text{EFFORT} = \text{SKILL}$$

$$\text{SKILL} \times \text{EFFORT} = \text{ACHIEVEMENT}$$

We often get caught up in the belief that leaders are born, not made. I hope the above formula shows you that this isn't true. Leaders are made, but only from putting themselves out there, making mistakes and learning, and falling down and getting back up again. Effort counts twice!

### Commitment

People with a high sense of commitment put everything they've got into the task at hand. They tend to find happiness and joy in whatever they are doing, often loving what they do.

I've no doubt that, if you're anything like me, you've been committed to something in the past… at least for a while. But then what happens? We lose enthusiasm for what we're doing; we wake up one morning and realise we don't have the same drive. It all just seems too hard, and we're no longer motivated by the challenge the way we used to be.

What's missing here is our sense of purpose! The reason why you're taking on this task. The reason why you spring out of bed in the morning and stay up late.

Duckworth identified our purpose, a clear and unwavering sense of *why*, as the focus that will keep us on course through the tough times. When things seem too overwhelming, when you feel that you can't go on, it's vital to remind yourself of your purpose; your reason why.

If that reason why is bigger than you, if it contributes to the wider community and goes beyond the self, then you will find the energy to push through.

Imagine for a moment if you were to commit to running a marathon. It's on your bucket list, and you convince yourself there's no time like the present! So, with your newfound sense of commitment, you bound out of the house and buy all the gear, shoes, socks, shorts, breathable tops, etc. In the beginning, the mileage is relatively low, and you ease your way into it. Buoyed by the sense of achievement, you continue to push on.

But then, the winter months roll in. It's dark in the mornings and dark in the evenings. It's colder now, and the wind and rain are relentless. You get the flu, and this stops you in your tracks for a couple of weeks. You try to get back into it, but soon get injured.

Finally, you realise it was all a bit of a pipe dream anyway, and you hang up your running shoes.

Now imagine seeing your son or daughter, your niece or nephew, lying in a hospital bed with tubes coming out of every part of their tiny body. The sound of the respirator sucking and hissing. The computerised *beep, beep, beep* of their heartbeat in the background as you pray that that sound never stops.

Your child, your niece or nephew, has a rare form of cancer of which there is no cure. Imagine reaching forward and whispering into that child's ear that you are going to raise money to help them get through this; imagine telling them that you will do whatever it takes to find the money. Imagine telling them that you will run a marathon, and you'll do it just for them.

Now, how insignificant are the aches and pains? How insignificant are the dark winter mornings, the rain and the wind? How insignificant are your injuries? Not one of these things is going to stop you from achieving your purpose. That's the power of having a clear purpose, a clear reason why. It's motivating, it's inspiring, and it will never, never, never allow you to give up. Ever!

Finding your purpose and effective goal-setting are key ingredients to developing a sense of commitment and overcoming challenges.

**Control**

People high in control believe they can influence events, especially their reactions to events. They take the time to think about how they can turn challenging circumstances into opportunities, are resourceful and proactive, and slow to admit defeat. This is known as having an *internal locus of control.*

People with an internal locus of control believe that they are masters of their own fate. They believe they can make a difference that they can find a way to turn off the noise or escape the electric shocks. The ten percent of people who never gave up in Hiroto's experiments had a strong internal locus of control.

The opposite of an internal locus of control is, of course, an *external locus of control.* A person with an external locus of control believes that their lives are controlled by external factors, things beyond their control.

Some examples of how people with these mindsets think are outlined in Table 7.2.

Ultimately, what Maddi and Kobasa found is that those who are higher in the three Cs score lower in depression and higher in:

- Happiness
- Self-esteem
- Energy and vitality
- Optimism
- Health
- Sense of meaning and direction

## Coach's Tip

Understanding that the three Cs make up a 'hardy' personality is one thing, but being able to apply them in the different areas of your life is another.

Table 7-2

**External v Internal Locus of Control**

EXTERNAL

WHY DOES THIS ALWAYS HAPPEN TO ME?

FATE BASED

WHY BOTHER TRYING? WHAT WILL BE, WILL BE!

OTHERS CONTROL MY DESTINY

I DON'T KNOW WHY BAD STUFF KEEPS HAPPENING TO ME?

THERE'S NOTHING I CAN DO

I'M A VICTIM

I TEND TO BE NEGATIVE, NOT TRY HARD AND GIVE UP EASILY

INTERNAL

I MAKE MY OWN FUTURE

FREEDOM BASED

MY PASSION AND HARD WORK HELP ME ACHIEVE MY GOALS

I CONTROL MY DESTINY

I MAKE MY OWN GRIEF, AND I CAN DO SOMETHING ABOUT IT

I CAN DO SOMETHING ABOUT THIS

I AM EMPOWERED

HOW I PERFORM IS UP TO ME

Pick an area of your life in which you'd like to have more resilience. On a scale of 10, how are you doing against each of the three Cs? What are you already doing that a Type C does, and what are some other things you can do to become even more resilient?

Focus on this area of your life for one week, then choose another and repeat the exercise, increasing your resilience in every area of your life.

For some specific examples on gaining more Type C attributes, next we will explore the…

# CHAPTER 8

# Strategies for Developing Resilience

*So I sat there, stewing over the ignorance of the man with the three-wheeler buggy, getting angrier and angrier.*

A few years ago, my wife decided to compete in the Sydney Marathon. With the training behind her, we arrived in Sydney and got settled into our hotel. On the morning of the race, Louise got up early and made her way to the start line. I followed shortly after with the girls in tow.

While Louise was out running the course, the girls and I decided we'd catch the train to the end of the race. We were waiting on the platform when the train arrived, and the doors opened automatically. I held my arms out, shielding the girls from the alighting passengers.

Suddenly, a man came charging through the doors, pushing a three-wheeler buggy right over my sandaled toes. I yelped in pain, but hurried the girls into the carriage before the doors closed. The train pulled off, and I sat there stewing over the ignorance of the man.

"How dare he?" I thought. "Everyone in Sydney is so rude! That would never happen in Wellington." I imagined myself running after him, grabbing him by the shoulder and giving him a piece of my mind. And if it turned physical, I was ready for him! The more I thought about the incident, the angrier I got. And the angrier I got, the more I thought about the incident.

If you've ever found yourself in a similar situation, where your thoughts run wild, making you angrier, sadder, lonelier, and disempowered, then the following pages will provide you with the strategies to move forward.

*When the negative thoughts come—and they will; they come to all of us—it's not enough to just not dwell on it... You've got to replace it with a positive thought.*
~ Joel Osteen

## I Think, Therefore I Am

Cognitive behavioural therapy (CBT) is one of the most widely used and successful therapeutic treatments in the world today. It's so popular because, quite simply, it works. It's effective in treating depression, anxiety, eating disorders, obsessive compulsive disorder (OCD), post-traumatic stress disorder (PTSD), and a range of emotional related issues.

One of the guiding principles of CBT is that 'everything begins with a thought.' However, because everything happens so fast, we often miss this link between the activating event (antecedent), and the consequential emotion or behaviour. This leads us to react as if forces outside of our control caused our reaction (see Figure 8-1).

Known as the Cause-Effect Model, it describes the idea that a person feels they have no choice but to be angry, upset, or scared, because something has forced them to be. The behaviour the person

Figure 8-1

**The Cause-Effect Model**

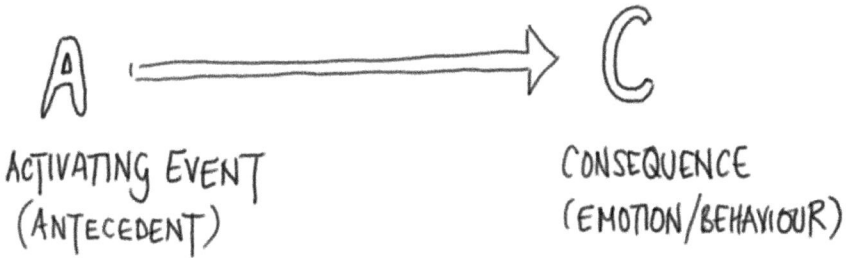

$$A \longrightarrow C$$

ACTIVATING EVENT
(ANTECEDENT)

CONSEQUENCE
(EMOTION/BEHAVIOUR)

---

exhibits is generated from a model in which they take no responsibility for experiences they could control. But this is not true.

Whether it's another person or situation that is causing us to feel a particular way, we must take responsibility for our emotions and behaviours. There are a couple of very simple cognitive models we can use to help us overcome this seemingly automatic reaction and turn it into a response of our choosing.

### Dealing with Negative Thoughts

We are all afflicted with negative thoughts from time to time, and they can bring us down and affect our mood and general happiness. People who struggle with depression and anxiety appear to have a constant battle with negative thinking and find it difficult to break the habit.

Figure 8-2 will be useful to you to help take back control of your thoughts, your emotions, and your behaviour. It outlines the model we're going to use in the following example.

So, to start, let's imagine that everything begins with a thought.

In this case, the recurring thought we're dealing with is, 'There

Figure 8-2

---

**The Thought-Outcome Model**

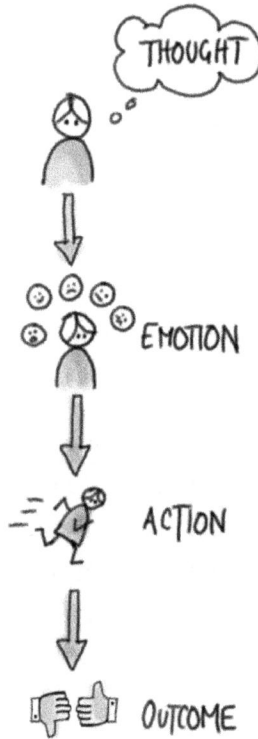

---

just isn't enough time in the day!'

If everything begins with a thought, and every thought leads to an emotion, what emotion might this thought lead to? For example, it could lead to feelings of frustration and anxiety.

Now, if every thought leads to an emotion, and every emotion leads to an action, then what kinds of actions might frustration and anxiety lead to?

From my own experience and those of my clients, these kinds of emotions can lead to procrastination and quitting. Let's consider what outcomes we're going to achieve from those actions. They are going to be stilted, delayed and rushed, poor-quality, or simply fail.

Here's what you need to know. If you're not happy with any of the outcomes you're getting in life, you need to change your thought. This isn't always obvious straight away, because we tend to jump from A (activating event) to C (consequence: emotion or behaviour). But with a little practice, it is possible to roll your mind back and capture your thoughts, however fleeting they might be.

Rarely does a single thought cause us to feel sad or angry. It's often a train of thought that intensifies the emotion. So, how do we

Figure 8-3

**The Thought-Outcome Chain Example**

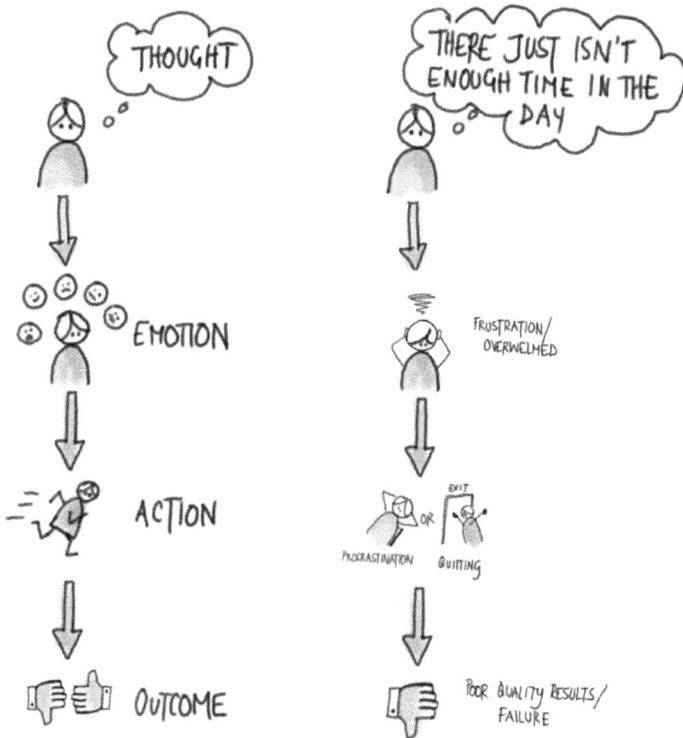

know whether to stay on the train?

It depends on how our thoughts make us feel. If we're having happy thoughts and they're lifting our mood, that's great! We want more of those! However, if our thoughts are making us feel a way we don't want to feel, we can jump the train. Our emotions are the key to developing our awareness around our thoughts and the impact they have on us and our performance.

I'd like you to do something for me. Go back to Figure 8-3 and block out the word 'Thought' in the diagram. What happens to the rest of the chain? That's right! It disappears. Therefore, if we didn't have the thought, we wouldn't have the outcome.

Similarly, if we create a new thought—something that is true for you—it will lead to a different outcome. Let's do that now. In Figure 8-4, my new thought is "It's not about time, it's about focus!" This leads to a sense of excitement, and I feel more energised. I'm keen to get started and take action, which leads to the outcome I'm really after: getting through the backlog of tasks.

**They're Not Your Thoughts Anyway**

In 1936, Carl Jung presented a lecture entitled 'The Concept of the Collective Unconscious' to the Abernethian Society at St. Bartholomew's Hospital in London. This is what he said:

"My thesis then, is as follows: in addition to our immediate consciousness, which is of a thoroughly personal nature and which we believe to be the only empirical psyche (even if we tack on the personal unconscious as an appendix), there exists a second psychic system of a collective, universal, and impersonal nature which is identical in all individuals.

This collective unconscious does not develop individually but is inherited. It consists of pre-existent forms, the archetypes, which can only become conscious secondarily and which give definite form to certain psychic contents."

Figure 8-4

**Change Your Thought, Change Your Outcome**

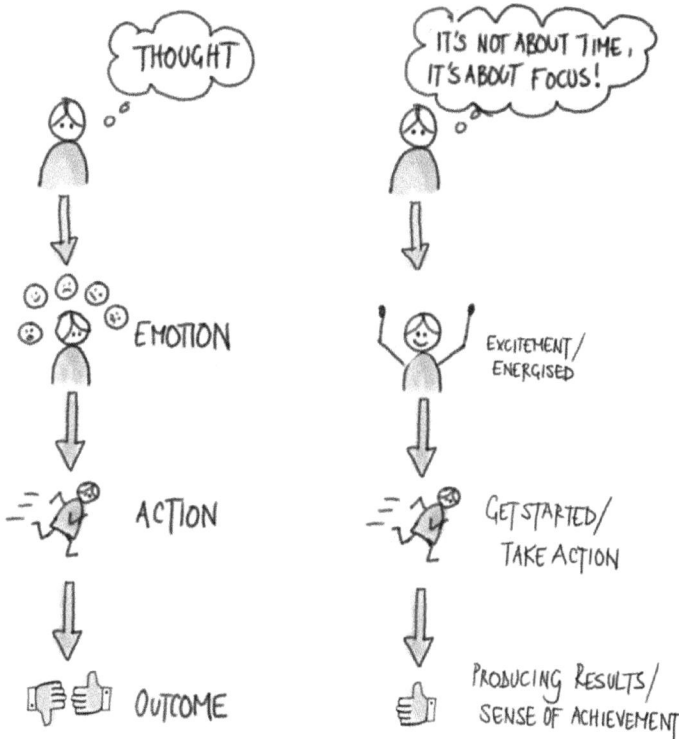

In short, the majority of our thoughts are inherited. They're not our thoughts. They belong to what Jung refers to as the Mind.

Do you think you're the only person ever to think that there just isn't enough time in the day? Do you think you're the only person ever to think that you're not enough? Of course not! These thoughts and this habit of thinking are passed down through generations, and are shaped over time by culture. They're not your thoughts! And if they're not your thoughts, you can change them.

**What's a recurring thought you'd like to put to bed?**

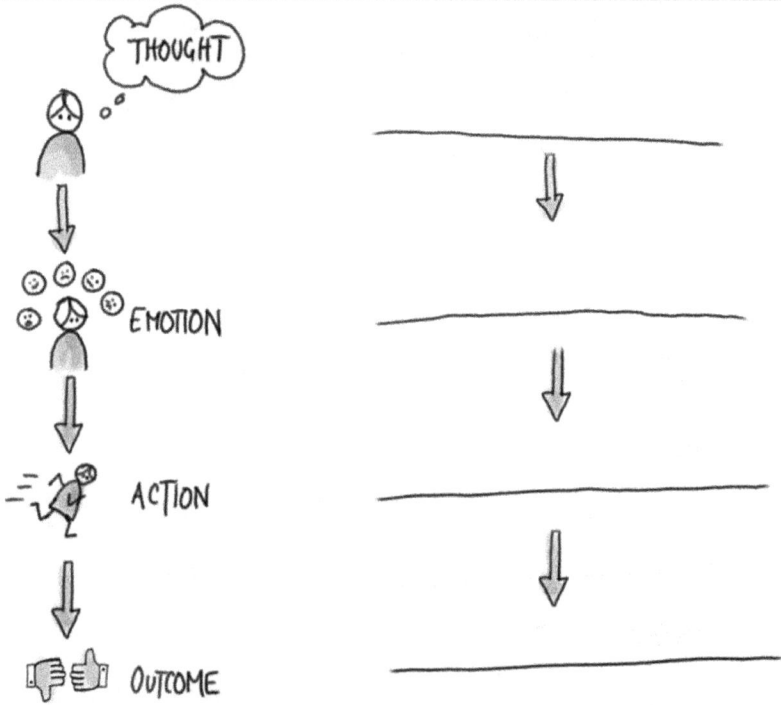

*It's as Easy as ABC*

Earlier in Figure 8-1, we introduced the Cause-Effect model. If you remember, this describes what happens to a person who takes no responsibility for their actions. They believe how they react, or how they feel, is outside of their control. Albert Ellis, a pioneering psychologist, recognised this phenomenon and developed the ABC

Figure 8-5

**The ABC Model**

A → B → C

ACTIVATING          BELIEF          CONSEQUENCE
EVENT
(ANTECEDENT)     ( THOUGHTS ABOUT )   ( EMOTION/ )
                 ( THE EVENT )        ( BEHAVIOUR )

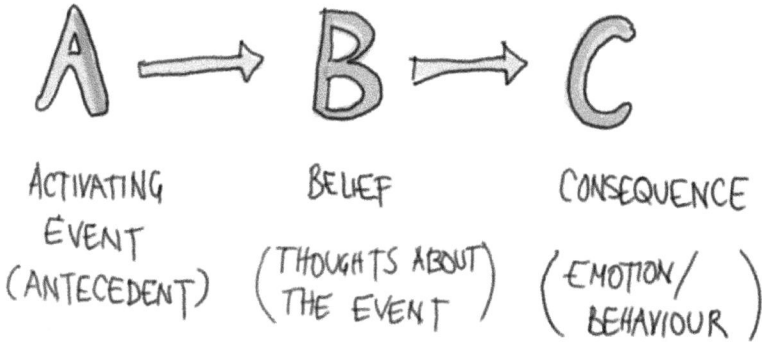

model to help clients determine the difference between rational thoughts and irrational thoughts. Let's explore the completed model now and discuss how we take back control of our actions and feelings.

As you can see from Figure 8-5, we've introduced the missing link: B—the belief we have about the activating event. This is where we can begin to take back control of our emotions and behaviours.

There are things in life that are always going to challenge us, but the one thing we can control is how we think about the situation—and therefore, how we respond in the situation.

The first step, as described earlier, is to catch our thoughts. Once we are aware of what we're thinking, we can start to challenge this thought. Remember, it's not your thought in the first place!

Figure 8-6 shows how we can do this.

*Resilience isn't a single skill. It's a variety of skills and coping mechanisms. To bounce back from bumps in the road as well as failures, you should focus on emphasizing the positive.*
~ Jean Chatzky

Figure 8-6

**The Complete ABC Model**

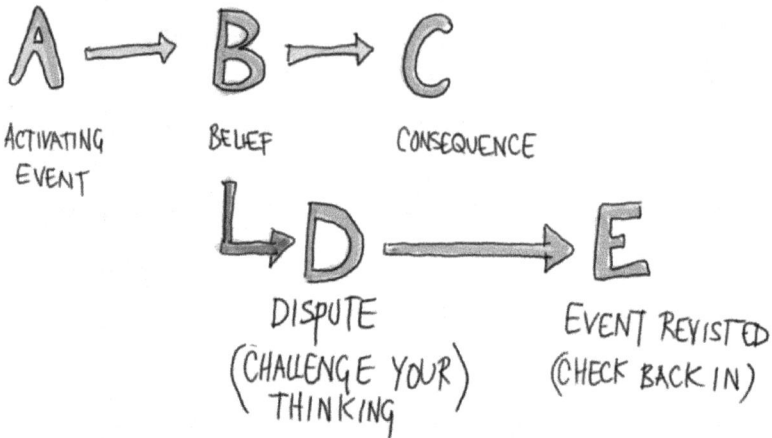

$$A \rightarrow B \rightarrow C$$

ACTIVATING      BELIEF      CONSEQUENCE
EVENT

$$\llcorner D \longrightarrow E$$

DISPUTE                  EVENT REVISITED
(CHALLENGE YOUR)   (CHECK BACK IN)
    THINKING

When we're aware of the disempowering thought (B), we can jump out of the existing chain and create a new one. We can introduce D and E into the equation. This is where our power is.

D stands for dispute or disputation. It's at this point that we start to consciously challenge the irrational or negative thought. There are several strategies to do this, and remembering them is easy. Just think about the vowels of the alphabet: A-E-I-O-U.

### A – Alternatives

What are different ways you can look at the activating event? If you're already feeling emotionally charged, the answer is probably going to be, 'None!'

But I want you to push yourself a little bit. Brainstorm some other possible explanations for the activating event. Maybe the person who cut you off in traffic didn't even see you. Maybe they had a family emergency going on.

### E – Evidence

Some people jump to conclusions based on the thinnest evidence. Take a moment to think about the event that triggered you. What evidence do you have that you should be upset or angry; how to you know your feeling is justified?

Sometimes it's only necessary to question the evidence you have for your immediate assumption before you realise it's a ridiculous notion in the first place.

### I – Implications

Consider the implications—the consequences—of the triggering event. Are you going to be late because one person cut you off in traffic? Is the world going to end? Are you going to get fired? Just because something you don't like has happened doesn't mean it's a catastrophe.

Earlier in the chapter on personal rules, we defined catastrophising as making highly negative predictions unsupported by evidence. Learn to de-catastrophise… the implications probably aren't all that bad.

### O – Options

No matter what the situation, no matter what the implications, you always have options. What are the things you can do to make it the way you want it to be? What resources do you have at your disposal to turn the event around? There is always a way to make a situation better than it is.

### U – Usefulness

The accuracy of your thinking may be spot-on. The situation might be dire, but if you brood on the problem now, will it do any good? For example, it would probably be a bad idea for a race car driver to think about crashing in the middle of a high-speed race. Being fully focused on the task at hand would be more useful—and help prevent the crash.

Therefore, it's useful to be able to distract yourself from negative thoughts. Martin Seligman in Learned Optimism suggests three simple but effective ways of doing this:

1. Distract yourself by doing something physical, like pinging an elastic band on your wrist or snapping your fingers, whilst saying to yourself, "Stop!"

2. Set aside a particular time for thinking about whatever it is that's bothering you. If you find yourself going back to the thought, say to yourself, "Stop! I'll think about this at 8 p.m. this evening."

3. Simply write down the negative thought as it occurs so you can attend to it later. If you have a little more time, why not go through the Thought-Outcome Model?

Lastly, E stands for event revisited. How has the event changed in your mind? How do you feel about the event now? My guess is, if you've done the exercise correctly, you'll feel much more at peace about the situation.

## Toe-Gate... Continued

So I sat there, stewing over the ignorance of the man with the three-wheeler buggy, getting angrier and angrier.

But then... I was distracted by my two girls singing and laughing on the train as they playfully moved the seat backs back and forth (Wellington trains don't do this, so it was a huge novelty factor). I looked out the window, and the sun was shining, portraying Sydney harbour in its best light. It truly was a beautiful day.

I started to dispute my thoughts about the earlier event. I asked myself about the alternatives; what else could the incident mean?

The first thing I thought of was that perhaps the man didn't even realise he'd run over my foot. My mind jumped to what evidence might support that, and I remember seeing the look on his face. He looked anxious and concerned, and maybe that's why he was rushing.

My next immediate thought was, 'I hope he's okay.' I felt the anger drain from my body, to be replaced with concern.

**Think of a situation when you found yourself ruminating on negativity and apply it to this model.**

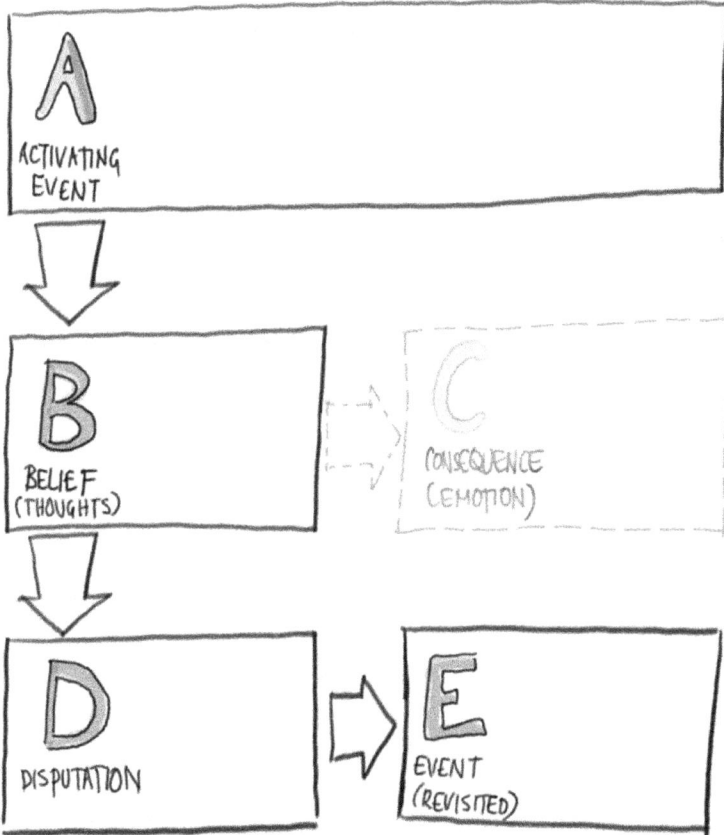

In total, that exercise took less than a minute. My mood instantly changed, and I got back to enjoying my morning with my girls. We met Louise at the finish line—she did great—and we had a terrific day.

## *Emotions*

Andy turns his head and, through groggy eyes, struggles to make out the meaning of the digits on his bedside alarm clock. The realisation hits him like a slap in the face, and he leaps out of bed muttering, "No, no, no."

There's nothing he can do. He's going to be late for the executive meeting he's supposed to be facilitating.

"How could I be so stupid!" As he angrily pulls on his trousers, he finds a $50 note in one of his pockets.

Smiling to himself, he thinks, "Maybe today won't be so bad after all."

Still rushing, he tears down the stairs and puts the key in the ignition. He turns it, but nothing happens. A dead battery! Slamming his hands against the steering wheel, he lets out an expletive that would leave Father O'Mara making the sign of the cross. Hastily, he calls a cab.

"There goes my fifty bucks," he thinks. He gets to the office to hear that the meeting was cancelled.

"Phew," he thinks as he slumps into his chair, smiling at his good fortune.

Shortly after, he receives a tap on the shoulder. He turns around to see his boss, clearly doing her best to hold back her anger. Andy learns that the meeting was cancelled because of his absence, which has reflected very badly on the team as a whole. His manager asks him to meet with her later that afternoon.

"This is it, I'm done for. I might as well pack my bags now."

A couple of hours later, a Human Resources representative calls him into a meeting.

"Here we go," he thinks.

She explains that his boss has been let go. Andy can't believe his ears. He does his best to stifle a smile as relief spreads through him.

"And due to this move," she continues, "we'll be performing a restructure. I wanted to give you an early heads-up; your role is being disbanded."

As Figure 8-7 below shows, Andy has had a very up and down day. What do you think was the driving force controlling Andy's emotions? If you answered the events of the day, you're absolutely right!

But Andy isn't alone in this regard. For many of us, our emotions are controlled by external factors. When something good happens, we

Figure 8-7

**Andy's Day**

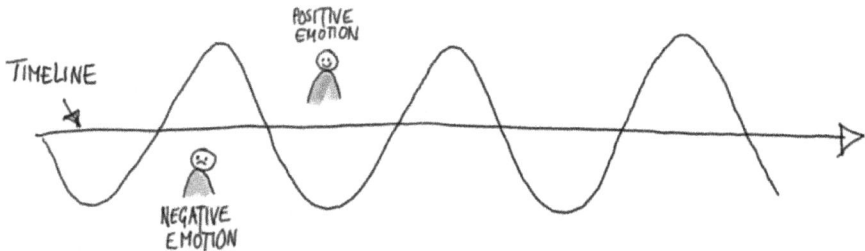

experience positive emotions. When something bad happens, we experience negative emotions.

But what is an emotion, anyway? In its most basic form, an emotion is a message. It is simply our brain's way of telling us there is something in the external environment that is at odds with our internal environment, and we should pay attention to it. It tells us that something is out of whack.

So, if an emotion is just a message, is there such thing as a negative emotion?

The answer is a resounding no. Remember, it's the meaning we put on these things that will determine whether they are positive or negative for us. We have a choice! Our emotions, like everything else our unconscious mind does, are there to support us. It's healthy to feel emotions, and we should pay attention to what they're telling us.

Of course, if an emotion is a message, we need to be clear what emotion we're feeling. Anger has a different message than hurt, for example, but these often get confused when we're in the moment.

Let's explore what some of the most common unresourceful emotions we might experience actually mean. Once we understand what they mean, we can put in place a strategy to move past them in a healthy and proactive way.

The first four unresourceful emotions listed below are those that have the biggest impact on our happiness and ability to move forward.

### Anger

When you feel angry or irritated, it means that either you or someone else has broken one of your rules. Clearly, I was angry at the guy who ran over my foot; what rule of mine do you think he broke?

This is a great one to use the ABC exercise on to determine if you have misinterpreted the situation. Does the person who broke your rule know they broke it? Do they even know it's a rule? How can you communicate that to them? Is your rule appropriate for this situation? Is it right for the context you're in at this moment? Asking these questions will help you reduce the intensity of the emotion and find a way forward.

*Anger cannot be dishonest.*
~ Marcus Aurelius

## Fear

Fear is certainly one of those emotions that sits on a continuum. It can mean anything from mildly apprehensive to absolutely terrified. The type of fear we're referring to here has to do with something coming up in our future that we need to prepare for. To release the fear, we must plan for the future.

Prepare for the situation and have faith in your abilities. Look to your past for the evidence you need to find the confidence to move forward.

The worst thing we can do is let our life be dominated by fears that cannot hurt us. It will lead to the regret of a wasted life.

## Regret/Guilt

Guilt can mean a couple of things. Firstly, it can mean that you have broken one of your own personal standards. It's your brain's way of telling you that you must do something immediately to rectify the situation.

Secondly, it can mean you're not living to your full potential; not taking action on the things you know you need to.

Therefore, the first step to removing guilt is to take accountability for breaking your standards, acknowledge that you haven't been living up to your true potential, and take action. Commit never to break this standard again (rehearse in your mind how you will act if ever faced with the same dilemma), and take action to start living your life how you want to live it.

## Hurt/A Sense of Loss

The emotions of hurt or loss tell us that we may have had an expectation that hasn't been met, either by ourselves or by someone close to us. We may have lost the trust of another person, or we may have lost trust in them. When you feel a sense of hurt, it's time to take a step back and ask yourself if, in reality, you've actually lost anything. Maybe you just need to reset your expectations and go again. If there has been a loss of trust, then it's important to communicate this with the other person; do it gently and empathetically… they may be hurting too.

When considering the loss of a person through their passing, a job, or a break up, ask yourself what meaning you're putting on this event. It's healthy to mourn, but is it for the right reasons? Isn't it true that one person might believe the person who died is in a better place, and this makes their passing easier to accept? Might it be true that some people get upset at the unfairness that someone passed away, or the sense of guilt for things unsaid? Take the time to fully explore the message of what you're feeling.

### Loneliness

All loneliness means is that you enjoy being with other people, and at this moment in time, you don't have that connection. So find a way to make that happen. If it's a connection with friends you miss, just picking up the phone will alleviate the need. Or if you miss the feeling of people around, perhaps a visit to a park or museum could help. You could also join a club or an organisation to meet other like-minded people that will help you forge new relationships.

Take the first step, reach out to someone, and make that connection.

### Unworthiness/Inadequacy

You may be taking things a little too personally here. This emotion is just telling you that you do not have the level of expertise required in a particular area… yet! Are your expectations correct? Take a moment to step back and analyse what you want out of a situation. Make a list of the skills and things you need to do to improve in the area you are feeling inadequate about. What resources are available to you to help improve? How can you learn them? Who can you learn them from? Once you determine the answers to these questions, create a personal development plan and execute it.

### Disappointment

Disappointment can occur when we have an expectation that is not met. Perhaps you fell below your own standards. However, there's a lesson in every experience. What's the lesson you can take away from this event? Or if it was someone else who disappointed you, perhaps your expectation of them was not set properly. What did you assume, and why?

### Overwhelm

Feeling overwhelmed means that you have taken on too much at once—you're overloaded. Stop and re-evaluate what's most important to you in this situation. (Your values are a good guide here).

Write down everything you have to do. Prioritise your list, select the first item, and take action on that. Move to the next item, and take action on that. Repeat this until you feel you are back on top of things.

Sometimes it may be necessary to just walk away and take some time for yourself. A holiday or walk can do wonders when you're feeling overwhelmed.

### Frustration

Frustration tells us that even though we're taking action and putting in the effort, we're just not reaping the rewards. It's a signal we need to try a different way of approaching the problem. In order to get the results we want, we need to grow as a person. Our current resources just aren't enough, but we know that they could be.

Similar to dealing with feelings of inadequacy, what are the skills you need to develop to put your desires into action?

Remember, your emotions are there to serve you. The message they're telling you shouldn't be ignored. If you try to push it down or ignore it, it will only intensify and come out at an unexpected time. Use your emotions to help you achieve.

## *Setting Yourself Up to Win*

When it comes to being more resilient, it's important to frequently push yourself outside of your comfort zone. Just like lifting weights, if you don't do anything, your muscles won't get any stronger. And if you do too much too soon, you could cause some damage. However, if you stress your muscles slightly, allowing time to recover before increasing the weight, they will adapt and become stronger.

The same is true for building resilience. Don't take on too much at one time. Just push yourself a little further each time, and assess your results.

Everything that we've discussed in the last few chapters requires effort. Coping with stress and building resilience is a process of changing your methods and evaluating your success. Coping methods are not automatic; they are a learned pattern of responding to stressful situations. And lastly, when coping with stressful situations, remember that your efforts should go into managing the situation (and your response to the situation), and not trying to control it.

## *Coach's Tip*

The last thing we need to consider is your allostatic load. Here are some proven strategies for you to implement into your daily routine to help balance your load. It's not necessary to do them all, but pick the ones that suit you best and turn them into a habit.

- Regular exercise
- Goal progression
- Optimism
- Journaling
- Friends and family
- Meditation
- Yoga
- Consciously balancing your 'must' and 'should' rules

Studies show that other people are the biggest cause of stress in our lives. But family and friends are also important to us, so we need to learn how to get the best out of our relationships. Therefore, we will now turn our attention to...

PART THREE

# Artful Communication

*The single biggest problem in communication is the illusion that it has taken place.*

*~ George Bernard Shaw*

# The Boy Who Would Not Be Broken

*O*ne morning, a young man was out walking with his father,
the village chieftain.

*"Father," the man said, "you look upset. What is it that troubles
you?"*

*The father looked at his son and explained. "Last night I had a
dream. I dreamt there were two wolves fighting in my heart. One wolf
represented hate, anger, and revenge. The other stood for peace, love,
and forgiveness."*

*The boy thought about this for a while and asked, "Father, which
one will win?"*

*The man responded, "Whichever one I feed the most."*

*It was then the boy realized, 'I have a choice!'*

*You see, for his whole life, he too had felt anger, hate, and
vengeance towards the surrounding villages. He had always lived in
fear of straying too far outside of the village boundaries, in case of
attack. But now he realised, he had a choice!*

*He determined that he would bring the villages together and
make peace.*

*That afternoon, the boy walked into one of the surrounding
villages and pleaded with the townspeople to come to talks and
entertain the chance for peace.*

*No one was willing to listen. One villager told him this had been tried before, and all it took was one stray word to cause offence, which led to more bloodshed. It was best left as it was.*

*However, the young man would not give up. He knew there must be a way. He didn't want to live his life with hate in his heart; he didn't want to live a life of fear. So every day he returned to the villages to plead for an audience.*

*Soon the villagers got tired of seeing him come around, and they started to beat him and chase him off. One evening, just before dark, he limped back into his village, beaten and bloody.*

*His friends, who saw him coming, pleaded with him to stop this madness. "They're not interested," they said. "You're going to get yourself killed... at least take a stick or something to defend yourself!"*

*Feeling sorry for himself and too ashamed to return home that evening, he walked into the woods until he reached a large pond. He made himself comfortable on a soft patch of moss under a large tree and drifted to sleep to the sounds of the resident frogs lamenting the end of another day. The next morning, the young man woke in the early morning sunlight. Still sore and aching, he searched the forest floor, picked up a stick, and headed in the direction of the nearest village.*

*Upon seeing the young man approaching the village, the villagers shook their heads in disbelief and clenched their fists as they went to meet him at the village boundary. Without saying a word, they raised their fists and were just about to unleash upon the boy when he shouted, "STOP!"*

*He said it with such conviction that the villagers were stunned.*

*"Wait," he continued, "let me show you how your strongest warrior cannot break this stick."*

*The villagers looked at one another in disbelief. The strongest warrior was in the crowd, and he stood forward, insulted by the challenge. "Where is this stick I cannot break?"*

*He reached forward to take it from the boy, but the young man said, "No, wait. Let me show you how you cannot break it."*

*With this, the young man bent down and picked up three sticks from the ground, one for each of the villages. He held them together and wrapped them in twine. When he was done, he handed the sticks to the warrior, turned and walked away.*

*The boy repeated this exercise at the other villages, and it wasn't long before the villages all started to work more closely together. They had realized, at last, that together they are stronger.*

# CHAPTER 9

# Problem Ownership

*I call them problems in embryo and they're largely unavoidable…
they just happen.*

The model of communication we're going to explore was introduced to me by one of the top Neuro Linguistic Programme trainers in the world, Richard Bolstad. It's called the Problem Ownership Model (Figure 9-1), and it is one of the most effective ways of communicating I have ever come across. There isn't a scenario I can think of that this model doesn't cover, and it does it in a way that provides the greatest chance of a positive outcome for all parties involved.

**We learned to communicate at around the same time we learned to walk, and that's probably the last time we've put any conscious effort into either of these fundamental skills.**
~ Cillín Hearns

Figure 9-1

**The Problem Ownership Model**

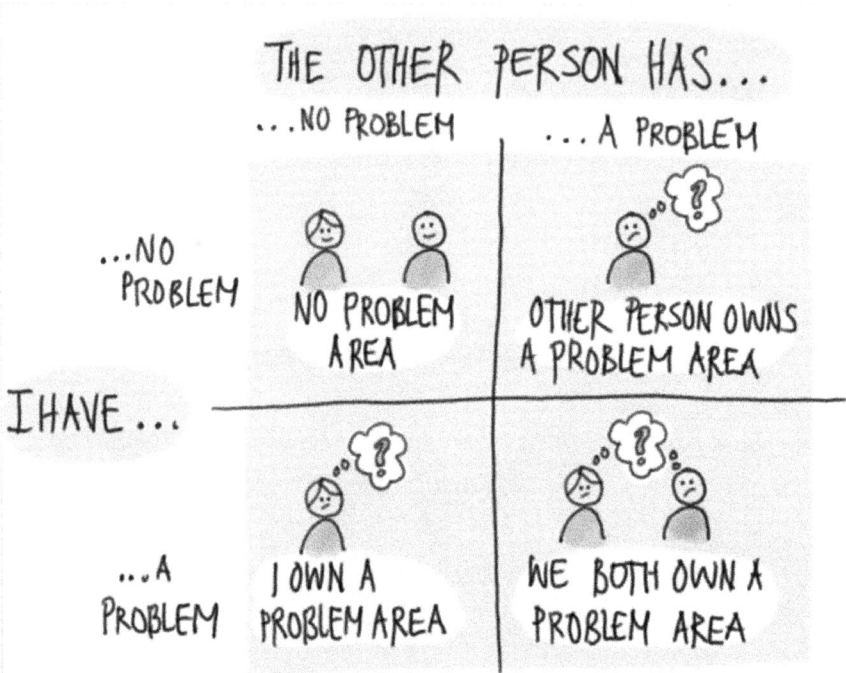

THE OTHER PERSON HAS...

...NO PROBLEM          ...A PROBLEM

I HAVE...

...NO PROBLEM — NO PROBLEM AREA | OTHER PERSON OWNS A PROBLEM AREA

...A PROBLEM — I OWN A PROBLEM AREA | WE BOTH OWN A PROBLEM AREA

The key to the success of this model is in the name. It encourages ownership of the problem from our side of things. We must take accountability for how we communicate. It's not about what the other person is doing or not doing; it's about what we're doing.

The problem with most of us when it comes to communication is that we do it unconsciously. We have to! To process the rules of language and the meaning of words, the subtleties of body language, tonal inflection, and so on would be way too much for us if we didn't do it at an unconscious level.

However, we can determine how we're going to communicate at a conscious level, and therefore not rely on the unconscious strategies we've developed for communicating during our earlier stages of life.

As you can see from Figure 9-1, the Problem Ownership Model is divided into four quadrants:

1. The "No Problem" Area
2. The "Other Person Owns a Problem" Area
3. The "I Own a Problem" Area
4. The "We Both Own a Problem" Area

All communication challenges (and opportunities!) fall into these four quadrants. The ultimate goal of the Problem Ownership Model is to expand the "No Problem" area, and hence reduce the problem areas in turn (Figure 9-2).

Figure 9-2

**The Goal**

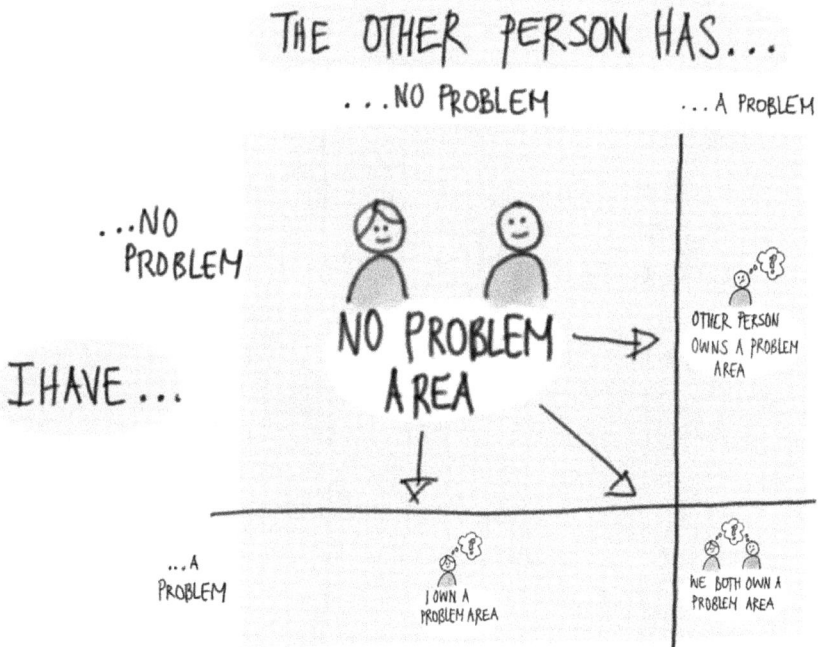

In order to achieve this, we need to focus on specific skills related to each quadrant (see Figure 9-3).

Let's discuss each of these quadrants in turn. As you work your way through each quadrant and practice the skills for each, it is important to recognise that the skills gained in each quadrant act as a bedrock for the success of later quadrants.

## The No Problem Area

In the No Problem Area, I don't own a problem and the other person doesn't own a problem. Everybody's happy, so why do we

Figure 9-3

**Skills to Achieve the Goal**

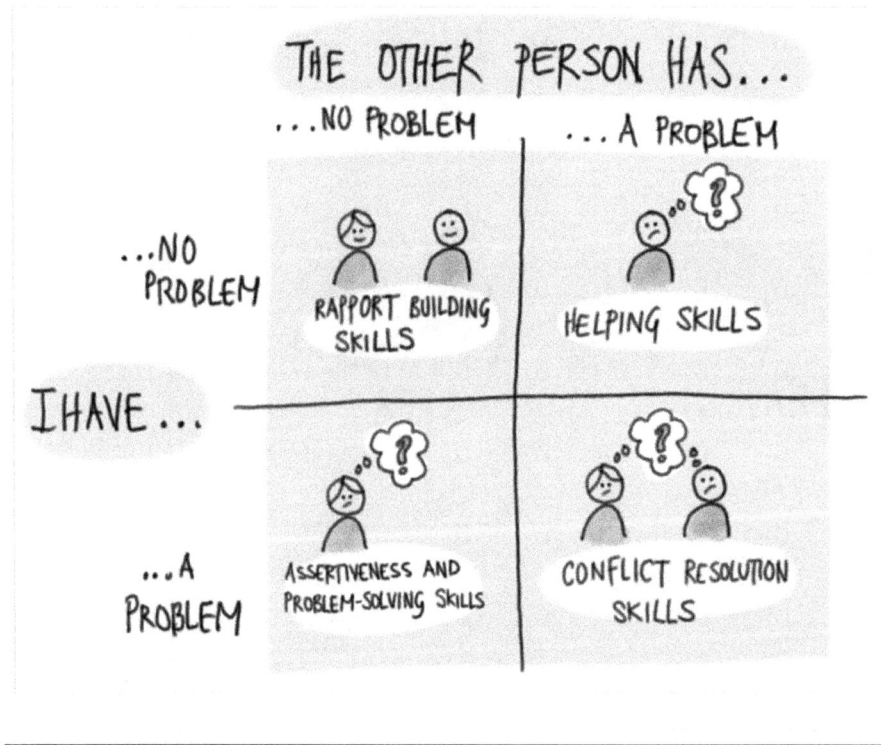

need to do anything at all? The reality of corporate life—or any other type of life where people interact—is there are going to be times where a misunderstanding occurs or a mistake happens. I call them problems in embryo, and they're largely unavoidable... they just happen. Therefore, we need to have some good will in reserve so that when a problem does occur, we have some capital to work through it.

In *The 7 Habits of Highly Successful People*, Stephen R. Covey uses a terrific analogy to explain this concept. He refers to it as the Emotional Bank Account.

Figure 9-4

**Rapport Building Skills**

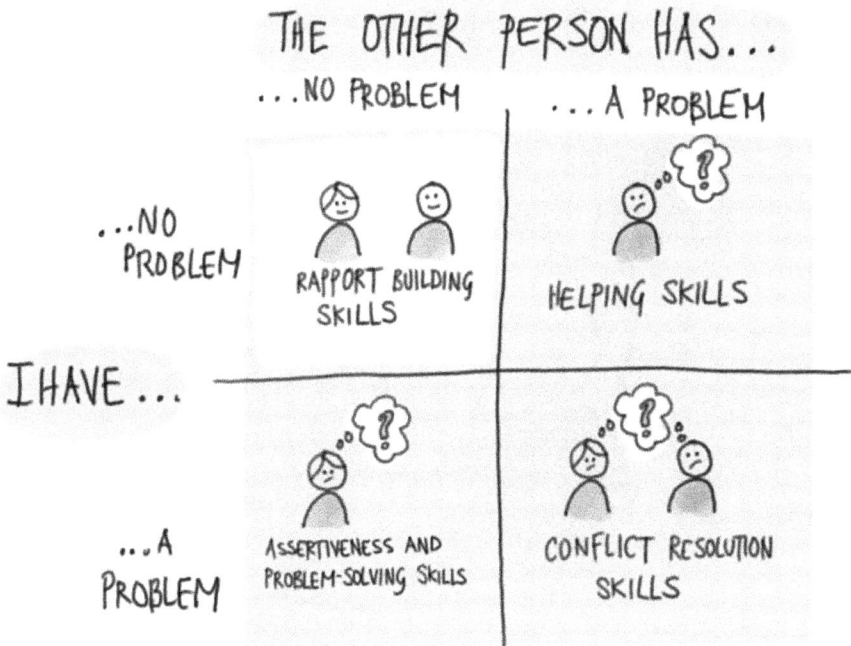

THE OTHER PERSON HAS...

|  | ...NO PROBLEM | ...A PROBLEM |
|---|---|---|
| I HAVE... ...NO PROBLEM | RAPPORT BUILDING SKILLS | HELPING SKILLS |
| ...A PROBLEM | ASSERTIVENESS AND PROBLEM-SOLVING SKILLS | CONFLICT RESOLUTION SKILLS |

## The Emotional Bank Account

Each of us has an emotional bank account with every relationship we have with another person. It works very similarly to a real bank account. If we deposit money, our bank account increases. If we withdraw money, our bank account decreases. Of course, when it comes to our bank account, the goal is to be in the black as often as possible. If we don't deposit money or withdraw money, our bank balance pretty much remains the same. Yes, it may gain some interest, but very little to impact things, if at all.

However, although the emotional bank account is similar to a regular bank account, it's not the same. If we deposit $10, our bank

Figure 9-5

---

**The Typical Bank Account**

THE MORE DEPOSITS WE MAKE, THE HEALTHIER OUR BANK BALANCE

NEGATIVE BANK BALANCE (RED)

POSITIVE BANK BALANCE (BLACK)

account increases by that amount. If we withdraw $10, our bank account decreases by that amount. This is where the emotional bank differs.

Let's use units as a measure instead of dollars. If we deposit one unit (have a positive interaction), our emotional bank balance (think relationship) will increase by one unit. However, if we make a withdrawal, our emotional bank balance will reduce by four units! That's right, the ratio for positive to negative interactions with another person is 4:1. Therefore, we need to have four positive interactions with another person to buffer against a single negative experience.

Many years ago, I was leading a big piece of work. We outsourced the technical component of the programme to a vendor who encouraged the use of an Agile approach to delivery.

This method of delivery sees the programme broken down into short iterations called sprints. An important part of this approach is the 'Morning Stand-Up'. This is a short, fifteen-minute meeting where people discuss what they achieved the day before, what they'll be working on today, and if they have any blockers to achieving their delivery goals.

Figure 9-6

**The Emotional Bank Account**

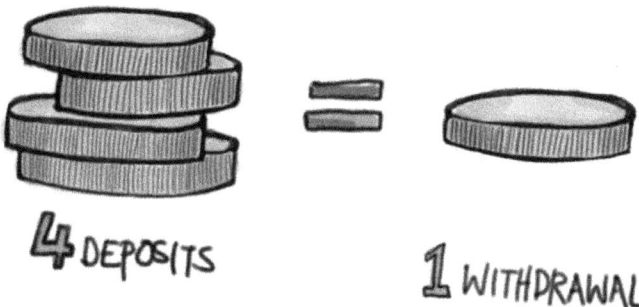

4 DEPOSITS          =          1 WITHDRAWAL

Since the vendor was only a two-minute walk from our offices, the business team agreed to hold the stand-ups there every morning at nine-fifteen. One Monday morning, I walk into work about thirty minutes late. I'm already feeling the pressure from the late start, and I'm emotionally charged.

The first email I read is from the vendor project manager giving out to me because the business team didn't show for the morning stand-up. With a heavy sigh, I banged out an email:

Hi folks,

Why didn't any of you show up for the stand-up this morning? How are the developers supposed to determine what to work on when you don't show up?!?!?

Do I have to walk you across there every morning to make sure you attend? Surely you can take responsibility for your own meeting schedule and show up.

Please don't let this happen again!

Kind regards,

Cillín

Now, this isn't exactly what I wrote (it was some time ago), but the tone was pretty direct and confrontational. Shortly after I sent the email, I started to receive responses such as, "What morning stand-up?" and "I don't have anything in my calendar."

I felt myself going pale and I checked the calendar. The recurring meeting invite had expired, and guess who owned the meeting request? Yours truly... major withdrawal!

Of course, whenever you mess up, you've got to own it. It's the only way out of it, so I immediately emailed a grovelling apology, reiterated my trust in them as a team, and praised the great work they've been doing (all of which was true). Shortly after, I started to

Figure 9-7

---

**My Team Emotional Bank Account**

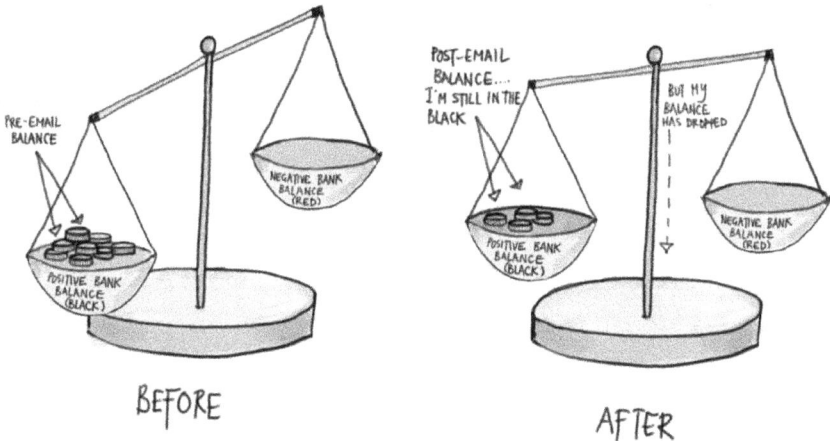

PRE-EMAIL
BALANCE

NEGATIVE BANK
BALANCE
(RED)

POSITIVE BANK
BALANCE
(BLACK)

BEFORE

POST-EMAIL
BALANCE....
I'M STILL IN THE
BLACK

BUT MY
BALANCE
HAS DROPPED

POSITIVE BANK
BALANCE
(BLACK)

NEGATIVE BANK
BALANCE
(RED)

AFTER

---

get little responses back: "Bloody Irish!" and "Glad to see you're human LOL."

Let's examine why it played out as it did.

I clearly messed up and made a huge withdrawal from the whole team. But the reason I got the responses I did was because even though I made a withdrawal, I had plenty in reserve because of my history with the team and them as individuals (Figure 9-7). I was still in the black, and I could recover easily.

Now, if I were one of those managers who didn't really care about his people and only focused on the delivery, if I never bothered to spend any time with the team, what do you think my starting balance would look like then? No doubt I'd sink deeper into the red, and it's likely my apology would fall on deaf ears. In fact, it's likely I wouldn't have received any acknowledgement for my apology at all.

So how do we build a healthy emotional bank account with others, and what are the things we need to avoid doing to prevent a withdrawal from occurring? Table 9-1 lists a few ideas to consider.

Table 9-1

**Examples of Deposits and Withdrawals**

| DEPOSIT ⇑ | WITHDRAWAL ⇓ |
|---|---|
| HELPING A PERSON IN THEIR TIME OF NEED | IGNORING PLEAS FOR HELP |
| APOLOGISING | REFUSING TO APOLOGISE |
| KEEPING PROMISES | BREAKING PROMISES |
| INCLUDING A PERSON IN DECISION MAKING AND ACTIVITIES | EXCLUDING THE PERSON FROM DECISIONS AND ACTIVITIES |
| SHARING A KIND WORD/COMPLIMENTING | BEING UNKIND AND DISCOURTEOUS |
| LISTENING WITH INTENT | NOT LISTENING |
| BEING LOYAL AND HONEST | BEING DISLOYAL AND DISHONEST |

The above examples are a great way to start building your emotional bank accounts, and I'm sure you can think of many more. There is, however, one way of increasing your emotional bank account exponentially, and that is achieved through how we respond to others.

## *Responding to Others*

Shelly Gable, professor of psychology at the University of California at Santa Barbara, has demonstrated that how you collaborate is more predictive of strong relations than how you deal with disagreements. People we care about may also tell us about a success or triumph.

Figure 9-8

**Responding to Others**

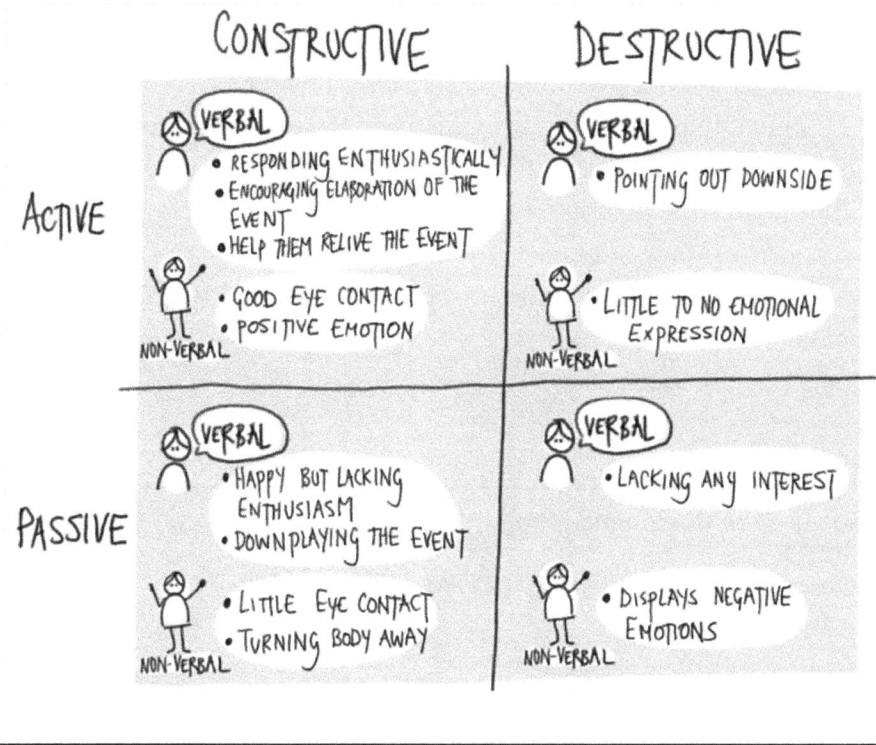

Gable stresses that how we respond can either build the relationship or undermine it.

When other people you care about tell you good news, how do you typically respond? There are four possible ways in which you can respond to the good events in the lives of others (Figure 9-8).

*Wise men speak because they have something to say; Fools because they have to say something.*

~ Plato

## *How We Really Communicate*

When I ask participants in my workshops how they build rapport, inevitably people talk about identifying shared experiences, such as hobbies or interests. While this is a useful way of building rapport, it is not the most effective. Let's take a closer look at why.

Three components make up face-to-face communication: verbal, tone, and body language. If each of the components together makes 100 percent, what do you think are the individual percentages for each component? It may not be what you think!

Figure 9-9 gives the correct percentage breakdown for how we communicate face to face.

Figure 9-9

**Face-to-Face Communication**

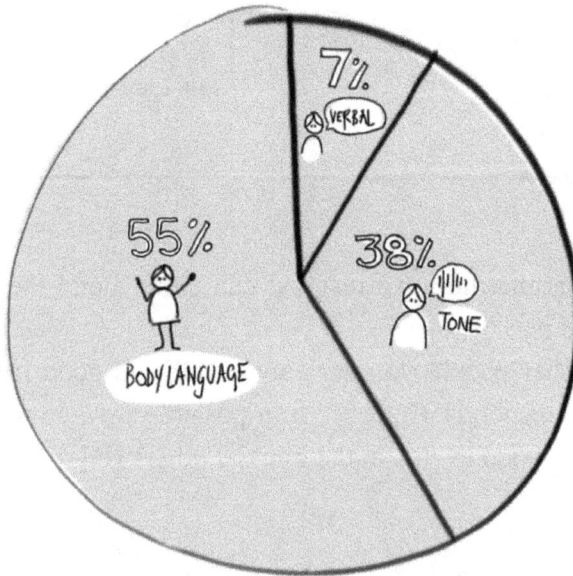

The fact that non-verbal communication adds up to 93 percent surprises a lot of people. So why is non-verbal communication such a dominant part of how we communicate?

Human language is estimated to have started to develop approximately 100,000 years ago, but our ancestors have been roaming the earth for about six million years. That's a long time! Therefore, although we have the ability for speech now, it wasn't always the case!

If you've ever visited the chimpanzee enclosure in the zoo, you'll know that you can very quickly determine who's agitated, who wants to play, and who wants a cuddle. We're able to determine this because of our ability, just like every other animal on the planet, to read and communicate effectively through non-verbal communication.

Therefore, to get back to my original question, the quickest way to build rapport is through body language... at least initially.

## *Mirroring*

Mirroring is the act in which one person imitates the gestures, pattern of speech, or general body position of another. It occurs naturally in social situations, particularly among close friends or family, and is performed at the unconscious level. We are often unaware that we are mirroring others or that others are mirroring us.

However, when mirroring occurs, it is a strong signal of rapport. At the neurological level, if you are mirroring another person, mirror neurons are activated within your brain, which leads to a deeper connection and understanding with the other person. This also leads to the other person who is being mirrored feeling a stronger connection to you.

Mirroring begins in infancy, as babies start to mimic others around them. This ability to mimic another person's actions helps the infant bond with the mother, develop a sense of empathy, and is the beginning of understanding another person's emotions.

Mirroring generally occurs subconsciously as people simply react to the situation. When two people in a situation display similar non-verbal gestures, they may believe that they share similar ideas and attitudes as well.

To sum it up, mirroring sends a signal to the unconscious mind of the other person that says, "You're like me, and I like people who are like me!"

As you can see from the examples in Figure 9-10, if the other person was looking in a mirror, they would see a similar body position reflected back at them. It's not necessary to mirror the whole body at the same time. Sometimes just mirroring the lower body or upper body alone is enough.

When mirroring another person, there are several aspects of body language that we need to be aware of.

Figure 9-10

**Examples of Mirroring**

*The art of communication is the language of leadership.*
~ James Humes

**Posture**

How does the person hold themselves? Are they slightly hunched or are they leaning forward? Is their body at an angle or are they standing straight on?

**Gestures**

Some people use a lot of gestures and others less so. It's not necessary to copy every gesture the person makes, but be aware whether they use them and mirror them as appropriate.

**Facial Expressions**

The person's facial expressions will give you an insight into how they might be feeling. Pay attention and reflect that emotion. Are they smiling and happy? Are their eyes lit up with excitement? What about their brow; is it furrowed with sadness or worry?

**Eye Contact**

Eye contact is a very important aspect of non-verbal communication. In the Western cultures, a lot of eye contact is considered good; it shows you are listening and you are a person of character. Eye contact isn't boring into the eyes of the other person, though. Good eye contact is considered general facial contact; i.e., your eyes can focus anywhere between the person's eyebrows and chin. In some Eastern countries, eye contact is considered rude (especially with elders), and should be avoided.

Lastly, you should avoid eye contact in prison… just saying.

**Proximity**

Proximity is the distance between you and the other person. Also known as personal space, it varies from person to person. If you get too close to someone, they will unconsciously let you know by stepping backward slightly. If they can't step backward, they will turn their body or head away just a little to give them more comfort.

Proximity, just like eye contact, varies among cultures. Generally, those cultures with high density populations, such as India or China, have a far reduced need for personal space.

### Touch

Some people are quite tactile in nature. They enjoy physical contact, whether it's placing their hand on your arm or going in for a hug. It's just how they're wired. If you want to mirror someone who is tactile, get comfortable with more touching… appropriate touching!

### How to Mirror

Some people are a little nervous about mirroring. They are afraid they'll be called out for it and the other person will think they're 'aping' them. In my experience, this is very rarely the case. If done right, people are completely unaware that you are mirroring them at all.

Obviously, you don't copy the person exactly; creating a gap between movements is important. The easiest way to mirror someone is to assume their position immediately; for example, if they sit down with their legs crossed, you sit down with your legs crossed.

People will naturally change position as they talk, and there are a couple of strategies I use to ensure the person is not overtly aware that I am building rapport through mirroring as I shift from one position to the next.

The first is to simply ask them a question or make a short statement. As they begin to respond, simply adjust your body position to mirror theirs. This works for a couple of reasons; the person is slightly distracted while they are processing what you have just said, and it's quite natural to change body position to reflect what you're thinking.

If my chin was resting on my fist, my head tilted up and my eyes looking upward, I have a good idea that you would say that I was thinking about something. Our body language reflects our thoughts, so it's perfectly natural to adjust your body position as you engage in a conversation.

The second strategy is to make a large body movement and then resettle. For example, taking a drink from a glass of water, scratching your head, or pulling up your socks—whatever is appropriate at the time. Then resettle in a mirrored position. It's as simple as that! Just keep it natural, and don't mirror any position you wouldn't normally use.

There are some situations when mirroring another person is not appropriate. For example, some women can cross their legs and wrap their foot around and behind their other leg. While this might be perfectly normal and acceptable for a woman to do, it might appear out of character for a man... but maybe not. Another example is if a man is sitting with his legs spread wide (as some men do), it would probably not be too appropriate for a woman to mirror this gesture... especially if she's wearing a skirt!

Lastly, you may come across someone who continues to change their body position once you mirror them. Ironically, not mirroring them is building more rapport than mirroring them! So after two or three times of them shifting, simply stop.

When I introduced the concept of mirroring, I mentioned it is the quickest way of building rapport with another person... initially. That last point is important.

Regardless of how effective I am at building rapport through mirroring, if we have a fundamental difference in our value system, the rapport will not last.

Imagine I'm building a strong rapport with Eliza, and I say to her, "Eliza, you seem like a relatively cool chick. What do you think about all this women's rights rubbish? Surely you'd agree that a woman's place is in the kitchen, eh?"

If Eliza is anything like my wife or my sisters, I'd be lucky to leave that conversation with all of my body parts intact! That's where the importance of investing in your emotional bank account is important.

Remember, be aware of people's preferences and own personal values. When they share with you something that they are excited about, get excited with them! Support them emotionally through difficult times, and listen to what they say. Keep your emotional bank accounts in the black!

# CHAPTER 10

# Helping Skills

*"You are the most ungrateful person I've met…"*

W hen another person owns a problem and I don't own the problem, the worst thing I can do is take ownership of the problem. Have you ever met someone who is insanely helpful to everyone else? They are often the last person to leave the office in the evening because they're doing everyone else's work as well as their own.

This is frequently the case for first-time team leaders. They want to do their best for their team, so they take ownership of their problems. Now while it's important that the problems be dealt with, it's also important to realise where ownership of the problem resides… with the other person!

The skills we need to develop to help the other person deal effectively with their problem are, put simply, helping skills.

**Words empty as the wind are best left unsaid.**
~ Homer

Figure 10-1

**Helping Skills**

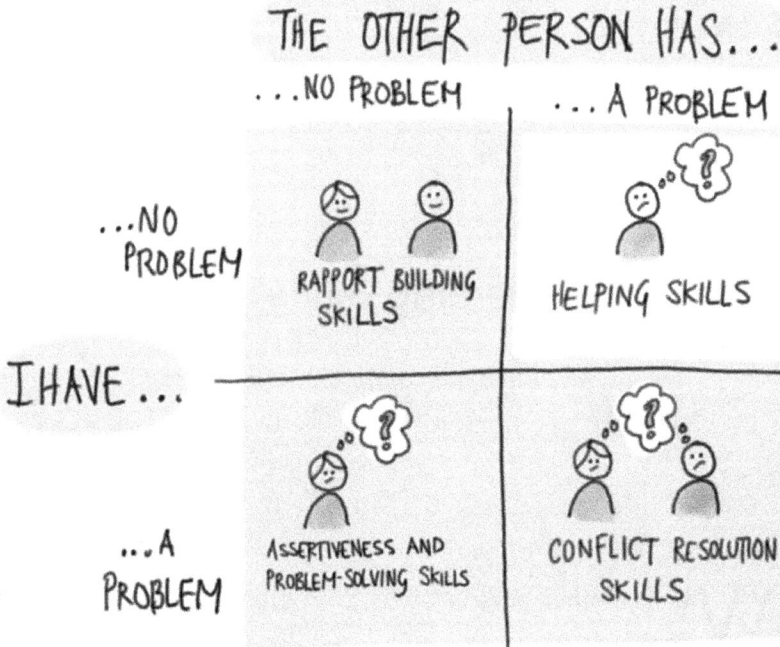

THE OTHER PERSON HAS...

...NO PROBLEM ...A PROBLEM

I HAVE...

...NO PROBLEM — RAPPORT BUILDING SKILLS — HELPING SKILLS

...A PROBLEM — ASSERTIVENESS AND PROBLEM-SOLVING SKILLS — CONFLICT RESOLUTION SKILLS

## Character First

Before anyone even decides to come to us for help, we have to have the type of character that people will seek help from. That's why being able to build rapport with people is vital to being able to effectively help another person; this quadrant builds on the foundations of the previous quadrant. There are several character traits people look for in a person whom they approach for help. Let's explore each of these and what they mean.

*Trust*

Trust is the belief that what a person is saying is what they believe to be true. This is closely aligned to the definition of sincerity.

But there is more to trust than just this. Have you ever had the feeling that you just couldn't trust someone to do something, but couldn't quite put your finger on it? The following breakdown of trust will help you articulate your feeling, and possibly lead to a positive discussion about your perception of the person's behaviour.

Not every question of trust is about a person's sincerity, and we should never question this aspect of trust. Questioning a person's sincerity goes straight to the heart of who they are—their identity—and a conversation like that will never end well. The other aspects of trust are as follows:

- Capability - You just don't believe the person has the skillset to do the work required. They may believe they can take on the task, so it's not a question of sincerity; it's a question of evidence of their current skills.

- Capacity - Have you ever worked with someone who is eager to impress and continually takes on new work, only to find, at the last minute, that they fail to deliver on their commitments? In this scenario, they are keen to help and they genuinely believe they can do the work, but they've just got too much on and can't do it all.

- Consistency - This is the type of person who one week is a rock star, but the next a complete letdown. It's difficult to trust someone who is inconsistent, especially on important pieces of work. Can you really take the chance?

- Quality - Some people have the attitude that good enough is good enough. In some situations this might be perfectly acceptable, but in other situations quality does matter. Does this person have that sense of care to get it 100 percent right every time?

- Vulnerability - Vulnerability trust is essential for a high performing team. Without this type of trust, people in the team won't put their hand up for help for fear of criticism, and they'll do their best to cover up mistakes and may even blame others. If you're a team leader, it starts with you. How can you show vulnerability and make it okay to be human?

## Honesty

Honesty is a component of trust and, like most character traits, it sits on a continuum. Where do you draw the line? Are white lies okay? Is it okay to tell a lie for the greater good, or do you believe that it's important to be honest above all else? Being honest with others also needs to be done gently. Remember, when giving feedback, the person may already hold the belief that they are not enough as it is; therefore, while it's important to be honest, be gentle and kind when communicating your thoughts.

## Integrity

Integrity builds on honesty and includes having strong moral principles; think values. A person of integrity isn't swayed by popular opinion if it goes against what they believe. A person of integrity knows their values and lives these every day.

## Caring

Are you the type of person who cares for others? If so, this will be obvious. Of course, it's easy to care for people who are genuine and caring themselves. It gets hard when the other person communicates in a less than cordial manner. Whenever I meet someone like this, I remind myself of the quote from *A Course in Miracles*, "Every communication is either a loving response or a cry for help." Can you see beyond the hurt? Can you see beyond the person's defence mechanism?

### Unconditional Positive Regard

Unconditional positive regard is a concept developed by humanistic psychologist Carl Rogers, and means accepting and respecting others as they are without judgment or evaluation. If we pass judgement on someone when they share something important with us, we will lose their trust immediately and they will clam up. If we want the person to be fully open with us, we must listen without judgement or criticism, and simply encourage them, in their own time, to share their thoughts.

## How We Listen

In *The 7 Habits of Highly Effective People*, Covey shares a terrific little anecdote about a man who goes to an optometrist. The man complains of tired eyes when reading and headaches after looking at a screen for some time.

The optometrist listens for a while, and then says, "Here, try these on," as he takes off his own glasses and gives them to the man. The man puts them on and finds them really uncomfortable; they make his vision blurry.

"No," he says. "No, they won't work for me." The optometrist is insistent.

"Try harder," he urges.

"These are awful," replies the man. But still the optometrist pushes him.

"What's wrong with you? Think more positively."

The man, getting exasperated now, says, "Okay, I positively can't see a thing!"

The optometrist shakes his head. "You are the most ungrateful person I've met… they work perfectly for me!"

If you found yourself in this optometrist's office, you'd probably get up and leave. All he's doing is prescribing his own glasses for you, even though you might have different needs. You might need a different prescription for your problem. But isn't this what we all do when someone comes to us for advice? Don't we all, with best intentions, give people advice based on our own experiences?

Covey calls this *autobiographical listening.*

### Common Barriers to Listening

Most people, when listening, are really only listening with the intent to reply. They're already formulating in their minds what they're going to say. They're just waiting for you to stop or take a breath so they can jump in and say their piece.

In order to respond to another person's problems, we have to interpret what they've said. And the only way we can do this is to filter it through our schemas (our values, beliefs, goals and our understanding of the meanings of the words they used). Therefore, we mostly listen autobiographically; and we've been doing this so long, we're not even aware we're doing it at all!

Covey tells us that there are five levels of listening:

- **Level 0 – Ignoring:** We completely block out the other person; they might as well not even be there.
- **Level 1 – Pretending:** We give the perception that we're listening, but our minds are somewhere else, isn't that right? "Yes, dear."
- **Level 2 – Selective:** If you've got kids, you may have experienced driving in your car while they're chatting away to you from the back seat. You're not really listening, but the odd word gets through: "Blah, blah, blah, crack cocaine, blah,

blah…" This, of course, gets your attention! The biggest problem with selective listening is we hear little bits and then make assumptions about the rest.

- **Level 3 – Active:** This is the level we've all been encouraged to reach. We are actively showing we're listening by making good eye contact and repeating back what you've said—but there is another level.
- **Level 4 – Empathetic:** Empathetic listening is the highest level. Through empathetic listening, we listen with the intent to truly understand the other person.

### Empathetic Listening

The key difference between empathetic listening and active listening is empathetic listening requires we express the emotion that we believe the other person might be feeling in this situation (Figure 10-2).

Figure 10-2

**Active versus Empathetic Listening**

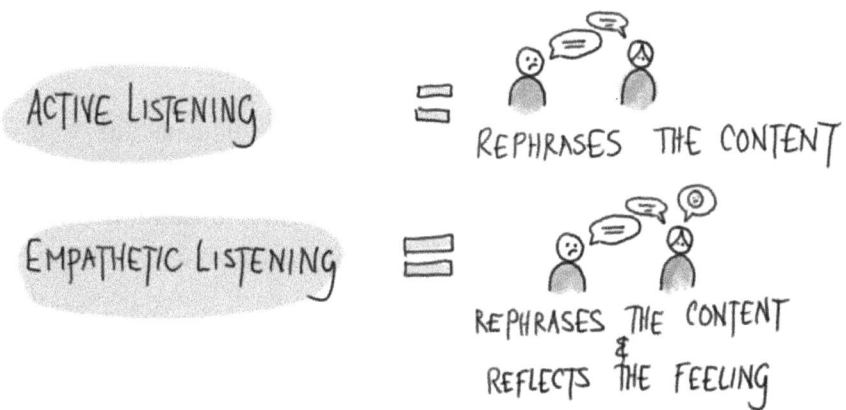

ACTIVE LISTENING = REPHRASES THE CONTENT

EMPATHETIC LISTENING = REPHRASES THE CONTENT & REFLECTS THE FEELING

Imagine a person says to us, "My damn laptop keeps crashing!"

If listening actively, you might say, "Your laptop is acting up." We've simply paraphrased back what the person has said to us.

However, with empathetic listening, we imagine what the person might be feeling and include this in our response. "I'd be really frustrated if my laptop was acting up like that."

It's important to remember to express how *you* would feel in that situation. If we say, "You must be really frustrated that your laptop keeps acting up like that," the other person may disagree, "No, I'm not frustrated. I'm just getting impatient because I've got all this work to do." This breaks rapport. However, they cannot disagree with how you would feel in that situation.

Before you run out and start practicing this in every conversation you have, please remember that empathetic listening isn't something that you'd normally use when you're on a night out with friends. It is contextual and, like every skill, is best used at the right times and in the right situations. Personally, I find it to be invaluable to reflect an element of emotion while communicating with someone. They feel heard, and when people feel heard, it turns into a nice deposit in their emotional bank account.

### The Art of Paraphrasing

Paraphrasing is arguably the most effective and useful tool in communication. It is very much underutilised in conversation, but is essential to the positive outcome of any important discussion.

When I ask participants in my workshops, "What is paraphrasing?" most of them say, "Repeating back to the person what they've said, but in your own words." That's a pretty good description, but let's expand on it a little.

Paraphrasing is especially useful when there is emotion involved in the conversation. Sometimes, especially when a person is feeling angry, frustrated, or upset, they can use a lot of words to describe what the problem is. If we try to repeat back everything they've said, we'd get lost in our words… it's just too much. Therefore, my definition of paraphrasing is, "Conveying the meaning of what the person has said in your own words."

To do this, rather than listening passively, we really have to try to understand what the other person is communicating by identifying the keystone of the message. A keystone is the final stone set into place in a masonry arch, locking the arch into position. Without this stone, the arch would collapse.

The same is true for a message. The meaning behind what the person is saying is the keystone, the most important piece. In paraphrasing, we are always listening for the keystone of the message. At the right time, we articulate that meaning in our own words. We know we've got it right when the person says, "Yes," and continues on with their story, often going deeper.

Paraphrasing helps the other person feel heard and meets their need for connection. Paraphrasing also encourages the person to go deeper, and that is extremely cathartic when the person is tied up with emotional turmoil.

Is it possible to go wrong with paraphrasing? Not really. If you paraphrase and the person says, "No, that's not what I meant," that's okay, because you get a second chance. The fact that you're trying to understand and showing that you're listening is what's most important.

## Listening with Interest

Paraphrasing is a vital tool for communication, but it alone isn't enough to demonstrate that we're listening with interest. To really show that we are listening with interest, there are a few things we need to focus on.

- **Minimal Responses** - These can be non-verbal like a nod of the head or use of expressions such as 'Mm', 'Mm-hmm',

'Ah-ha', 'I see', 'Sure', 'Right', 'Oh', 'Really'. Remember to insert these at regular intervals and space appropriately. If they are used too frequently, they will come across as intrusive. If they aren't used frequently enough, we may appear to be inattentive.

- **Brief invitations to continue** - Sometimes, the person will pause while speaking, thinking or perhaps waiting for encouragement to go on. When you think they're ready to continue, it is useful to give a brief invitation such as 'Then...', 'And...', 'Tell me more...', 'What else...' and so on.
- **Non-verbal behaviour** - We've already covered these under body language. To recap, non-verbal behaviour includes physical closeness (proximity), gestures, facial expression, eye contact, and so on.
- **Voice** - Clarity and volume are key aspects of the voice, as is speed of speaking and, of course, tone.
- **Silence** - Silence can be very powerful, especially after asking an open-ended question and when a person is quite emotional. It is important to continue to use appropriate eye contact so that you are seen to be listening with a high level of interest.

## Masterful Questioning

Asking questions is another important component to helping a person solve their problem. Used correctly, good questioning can guide the person to the solution or help them go deeper to access resources that they haven't drawn on for quite some time. Although there are many types of questions, all questions fall into one of two camps:

- Open Questions
- Closed Questions

## *Open Questions*

We use open questions to understand more about a situation or the other person's thinking/reasoning. In short, we use open questions to gather information. The types of open question words include:

- Who
- What
- When
- Why

- Where
- How
- How often
- How come

All of the above are useful in opening up a conversation to try and find out more about a person or a situation. However, 'why' type questions should be avoided as much as possible. Whilst, on the surface, they appear to be useful for understanding the person's motives, they can also sound confrontational and lead to a defensive response. Essentially, you're asking the person to defend the position they hold or the actions they have taken rather than discussing what's important about those positions and actions.

A question as simple as "Why did you do it that way?" could be interpreted as "You messed up, you did it wrong!" Instead of asking "Why did you do it that way?" you could ask "What led you to take that course of action?" This subtle but powerful difference can greatly impact the listener and the outcome of the conversation.

*Sometimes, all that's needed is to listen and to be kind.*
~ Cillín Hearns

Table 10-1

**Possible Alternatives to 'Why' Questions**

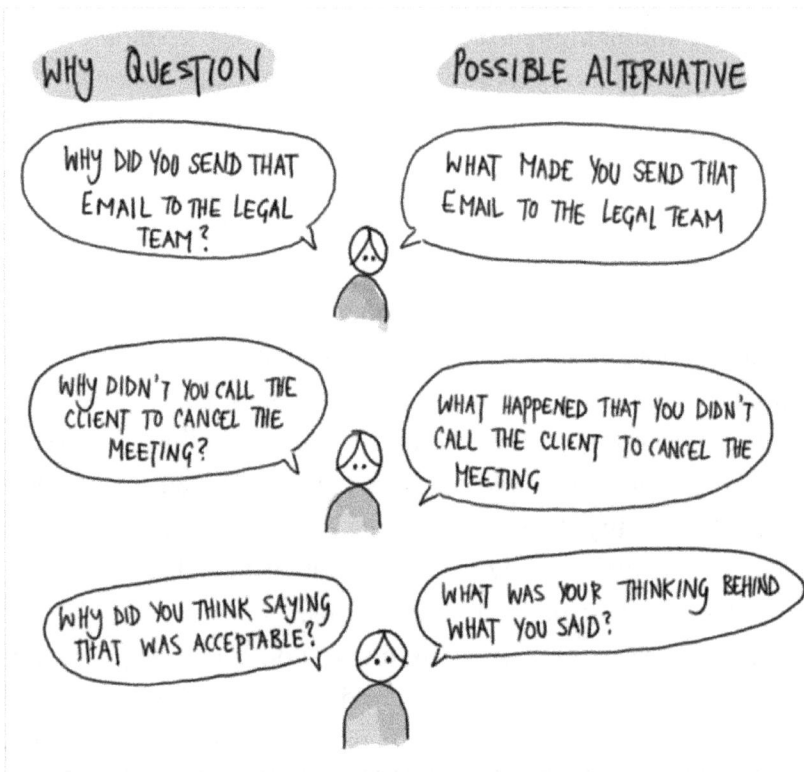

| WHY QUESTION | POSSIBLE ALTERNATIVE |
|---|---|
| WHY DID YOU SEND THAT EMAIL TO THE LEGAL TEAM? | WHAT MADE YOU SEND THAT EMAIL TO THE LEGAL TEAM |
| WHY DIDN'T YOU CALL THE CLIENT TO CANCEL THE MEETING? | WHAT HAPPENED THAT YOU DIDN'T CALL THE CLIENT TO CANCEL THE MEETING |
| WHY DID YOU THINK SAYING THAT WAS ACCEPTABLE? | WHAT WAS YOUR THINKING BEHIND WHAT YOU SAID? |

## *Closed Questions*

The purpose of closed questions is to gain agreement or closure, to confirm certain aspects of the conversation, or to confirm your understanding. Isn't that right? Sorry, I couldn't help myself (chuckle). The types of closed question words include:

- Are
- Did
- Have
- Could
- Is
- Do
- Can
- Will
- Does

Both are useful in a conversation and should be used at the right times. Before asking a question, consider the outcome you hope for or the information you want to discover. A concern that should always be forefront in your mind is, "How can I empower this person and make them feel safe in this conversation?"

## *Questioning Tips*

1. Always pause between questions to prevent the other person from feeling interrogated. It's useful to ask a question, paraphrase, and then ask another question if you're looking to get to the bottom of something.
2. Let your questions flow naturally based on the developing conversation. Your questions should be relevant and, as mentioned above, leading towards an outcome.
3. Keep your questions short, sharp and precise. Long, drawn out questions can cause confusion. Keep them simple and on point.
4. Using endless open-ended questions in an area where the other party has little knowledge will put unwanted pressure on them (as will early use of 'why' questions, if you must use them).
5. When using open-ended questions, always follow with silence. Allow the person to answer the question, and don't answer it for them! Give them a chance to consider what you're asking, and let them respond.

Identify the presupposition (what has to be true) behind the following questions and the information being sought (the real intent behind the question). How could you improve on these?

**Question:**          Have you completed the requirements document?

**Presupposition:**    *The person should have already completed it.*

**Intent:**            *To understand the progress of the requirements document.*

**Improvement:**       *How's that requirements document coming along?*

---

**Question:**          Do you know the reason for that?

**Presupposition:**    _____

_____

**Intent:**            _____

_____

**Improvement:**       _____

_____

---

**Question:**          Why did you do it that way?

**Presupposition:**    _____

_____

**Intent:**            _____

_____

**Improvement:** _____

_____

---

**Question:**        Where's the document I asked you for?

**Presupposition:** _____

_____

**Intent:**          _____

_____

**Improvement:**     _____

_____

---

**Question:**        Why did you not finish the report before you left?

**Presupposition:** _____

_____

**Intent:**          _____

_____

**Improvement:**     _____

# CHAPTER 11

_____

# Assertiveness and Problem-Solving Skills

*"John, I'd like to talk to you about your behaviour in the meeting when you yelled at everybody, slammed your pen onto the desk and stormed out of the meeting room."*

When I own the problem and the other person doesn't own a problem, it's important that I'm able to communicate that I have a problem to the person in a respectful and professional manner. In order to do this, it's important to be able to assert your point of view.

## Assertiveness

Assertiveness is often viewed as a personality trait, and we'll be looking more into this when we explore Working Style Profiles in the next chapter. However, although it is a personality trait, it can also be wielded as a skill when necessary and in the right context.

Figure 11-1

**Assertive and Problem-Solving Skills**

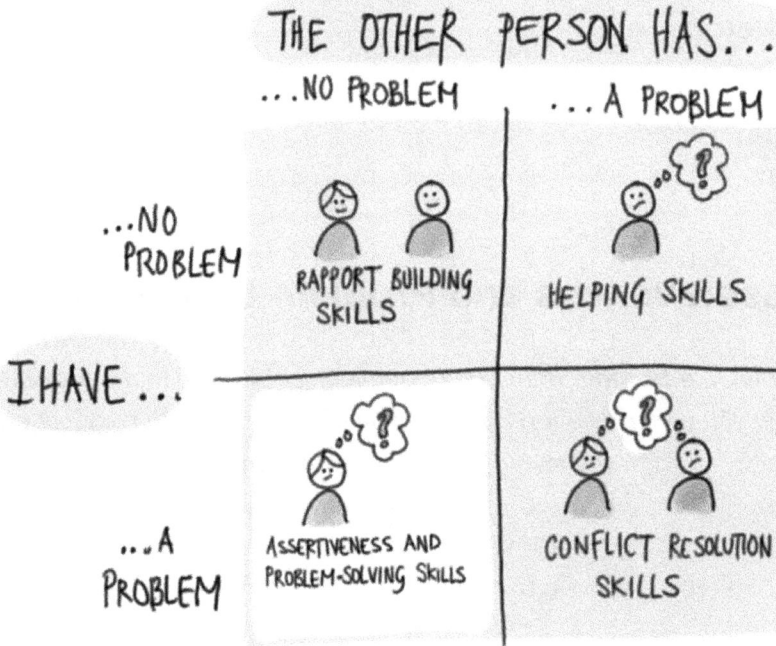

*Wise men speak because they have something to say; Fools because they have to say something.*
~ Plato

In Figure 11-2, we see that the Assertiveness Curve has three stages: Passive, Assertive, and Aggressive.

Figure 11-2

**The Assertiveness Curve**

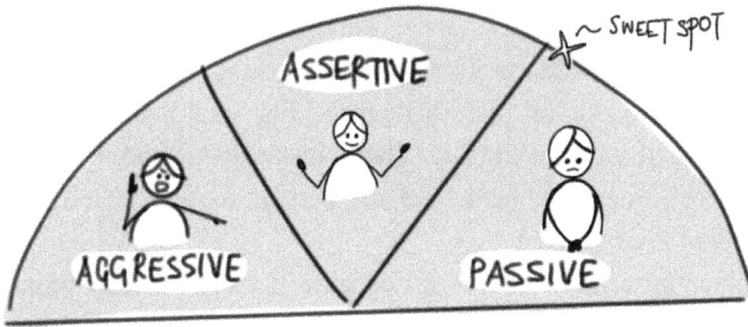

It's my view that there is no place for aggressive behaviour in the business environment. There just simply isn't. If you find that you are drawn to aggressiveness, I would suggest understanding your emotional triggers (see the chapter on Rules to get a better understanding of what these might be), implementing your strategies for managing stress, and focusing on developing your communication and influencing skills, so you get more of what you want.

My preferred position on the Assertiveness Curve is high in the passive range. Too low in the passive range, and you can come across as wishy-washy. This can be frustrating for some people, especially Driver-style personalities, which we'll explore more in the next chapter.

A person high on the passive range tends to use questions over commands. For example, rather than stating, "Send me the document by the end of the day," we could say, "Would you mind sending me the document by the end of the day?" You are likely to get the same outcome, and it's a much more pleasant message for the person on the receiving end.

In every organisation, there is an implicit hierarchy. Therefore, as a leader, it's not necessary to exert your authority. Even if you're not in a leadership position, people are much more likely to respond favourably if you ask rather than command.

This approach works very well in most situations, but there may come a time when it's necessary to move up the dial into the assertive range. If your gentle approach isn't working, being respectfully assertive can make all the difference. For example, "I need the document by the end of the day. Please ensure you send it to me" is a much more direct statement, and the person should be left with no doubt about your request.

This approach works so well because if you're mostly passive in your communications and go into assertive, people stand up and take note. However, if you're always assertive, where can you go? That's right, you can only head towards the aggressive range.

In business, as well as in life, you can't control people, you can only influence. You may be able to get what you want in the short term through your demands, but this often leads to breakdown in trust, massive withdrawals from the emotional bank account, and relationship complications in the long term.

One of the key aspects of assertiveness is that it should be about what *you* want. If you need to communicate a problem (that you own!) to another person, it should be delivered in an 'I' statement.

## The 'I' Statement

The 'I' statement is an assertive way of communicating a problem that you own. Using an 'I' statement has several advantages over other reactive-type communications.

### What Does an 'I' Statement Do?

An effective 'I' statement does several things:

- It preserves the quality of the relationship. When two people in a relationship don't communicate their needs and annoyances, it can lead to resentment. Resentment is the main emotion that leads to relationship breakdowns.

- It helps the other person understand you. By communicating your problems or displeasures, the other person gets to know your preferences or boundaries.
- It protects the self-esteem of the other person. Because, as we'll see in a moment, since an 'I' statement comes from your perspective (it's less about the other person), the person is less likely to be affronted by your communication.
- It has a high chance of changing unacceptable behaviour. This is because the message is clear and delivered respectfully.

## *The Structure of an 'I' Statement*

An 'I' statement is made up of the following components:

- A sensory-specific description of the **behaviour**, a description of what actually happened.
- The actual, concrete, tangible **effects** of that behaviour on **me**.
- How I **feel** about the behaviour and its effects.

I've found the best way to construct an 'I' statement is to break it into its component parts. Let's use the following example:

- **BEHAVIOUR** - The person didn't do the dishes as previously arranged.
- **EFFECTS** - I end up doing them at a time when I want to use the countertop.
- **FEELINGS:** Unhappy, frustrated.

The fully constructed 'I' statement would read:

*"When you don't do the dishes you've arrange to do, I end up needing to do them in order to use the bench, and I dislike the extra work."*

This could be further improved by removing the 'you' reference in the above statement. The word 'you' personalises the statement, which may lead to defensive behaviour. We want to avoid this as much as possible, because the purpose of the 'I' statement is to open up the conversation and invite the person into the conversation in a constructive manner. Therefore, the above 'I' statement could be improved by changing it to:

*"When the dishes aren't done as we've arranged, I end up needing to do them in order to use the bench, and I dislike the extra work."*

This is less direct, but I imagine the other person will understand the implication behind the message: they aren't pulling their weight.

Let's explore the 'I' statement a little more. The importance of using an 'I' statement cannot be overstated, because the first sentence we use in a potentially conflicting conversation will determine whether the outcome of that conversation will be a success or a failure.

Research from The Gottman Institute tells us that if we get the first sentence incorrect (i.e., it causes a negative emotional response in the other person), we have about a five percent chance of turning that conversation around. That's why taking the time to structure your opening statement is so important.

Therefore, we need to pay particular attention to the sensory-specific description of the behaviour we observed to ensure we are as neutral and as factual in the description as possible. For example, if you observe someone shouting in a meeting, slamming their pen onto the table and storming out of the room, leaving everyone shocked and unsure what to do next, how would you communicate this to them?

Let's have a go:

*"John, I'd like to talk to you about your behaviour in the meeting when you yelled at everybody, slammed your pen onto the desk and stormed out of the meeting room* [behaviour]. *You were clearly very angry and upset and it left everybody unsettled* [effect], *and I felt a little scared at witnessing such a display* [feeling]. *"*

How do you think that conversation is going to go? Although the structure of the statement is largely correct, you can imagine John getting defensive straight away.

If we feel we are being attacked—physically or emotionally—our brains respond accordingly by triggering the sympathetic nervous system, causing a fight-or-flight response. The average resting heartrate of a person is 72 bpm, so if our heartrate rises above 95 bpm, we will act as if we are truly under attack, and our responses are more likely to be emotive rather than rational.

Figure 11-3

**The Body's Physiological Response to Attack**

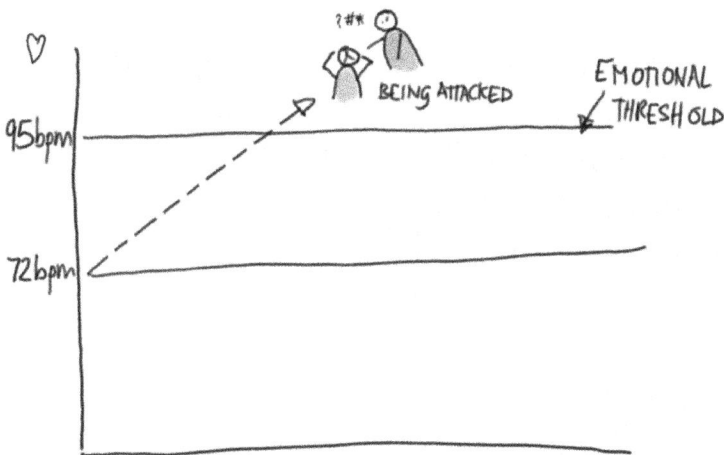

So how can we address this problem whilst minimising the negative response? The secret is in identifying the emotive language and the inferences we make in the sensory-specific observed behaviour. Can you spot them? Let's break them down (see Table 11-1).

The purpose behind the possible alternatives listed above is to try and neutralise the language as much as possible. It's important not to downplay the message and equally important not to trigger the person straight away. The inferences should be excluded from your statement, because they are an assumption of how you might be feeling if you displayed that behaviour. It may not be true for the other person.

Table 11-1

**Emotive Language and Inferences**

| BEHAVIOUR | CATEGORY | POSSIBLE ALTERNATIVE |
|---|---|---|
| ... YELLED AT EVERYBODY | EMOTIVE DESCRIPTOR | ... RAISED YOUR VOICE |
| ... SLAMMED YOUR PEN | EMOTIVE DESCRIPTOR | ... PLACED YOUR PEN DOWN HARD |
| ... STORMED OUT | EMOTIVE DESCRIPTOR | ... WALKED OUT QUICKLY |
| ... VERY ANGRY | INFERENCE | |
| ... UPSET | INFERENCE | |

Therefore, our new 'I' statement would be:

*"John, I'd like to talk to you about what happened in the meeting when you raised your voice, placed your pen down hard on the desk and walked quickly out of the room* [behaviour]. *It left everybody feeling unsettled* [effect], *and I felt a little scared from what I saw* [feeling]. *"*

Although John might feel uncomfortable about being confronted by his behaviour, this statement is unlikely to trigger a strong negative reaction.

## Dealing with Resistance

Earlier, we mentioned that the Helping Skills quadrant builds on the Rapport-Building Skills quadrant. The same is true of the Assertiveness and Problem-Solving Skills. In fact, Assertiveness and Problem-Solving Skills and Helping Skills go hand in hand. Here's why.

Communication is rarely as straightforward as delivering an 'I' statement and the problem is solved. In most cases, the person is going to respond with resistance, falling back on old habits of feeling that they haven't been heard and focusing only on getting their point across. But we're not going to do that, are we? We're going to take the person on a conversational dance.

If the person objects to what we say, we simply paraphrase what they said and seek to understand their point of view (see Figure 11-4).

*Words are singularly the most powerful force available to humanity. We can choose to use this force constructively with words of encouragement, or destructively using words of despair. Words have energy and power with the ability to help, to heal, to hinder, to hurt, to harm, to humiliate and to humble.*
~ Yehuda Berg

Figure 11-4

**The Conversational Dance**

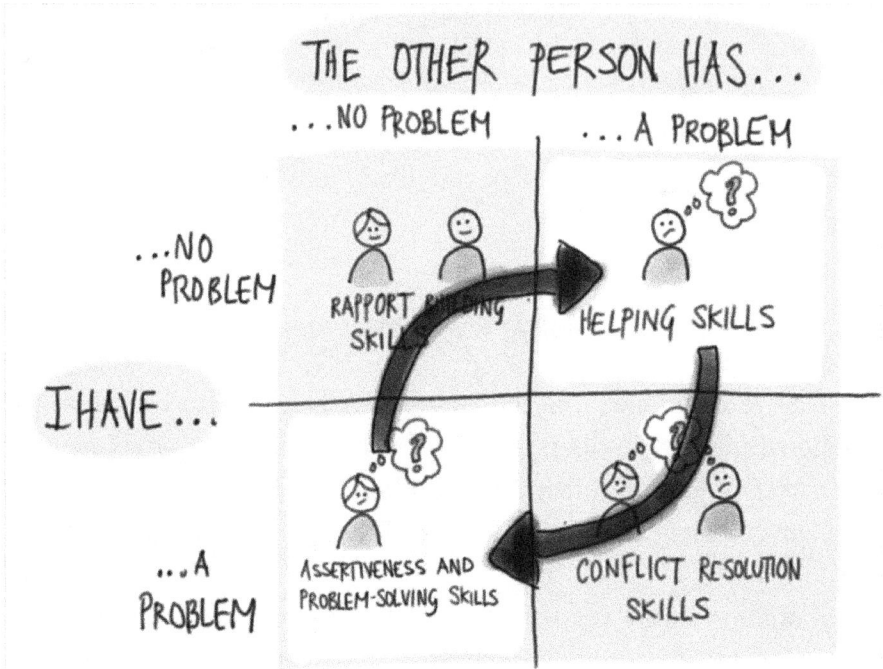

THE OTHER PERSON HAS...

...NO PROBLEM ...A PROBLEM

...NO PROBLEM — RAPPORT BUILDING SKILLS

...A PROBLEM — HELPING SKILLS

I HAVE...

ASSERTIVENESS AND PROBLEM-SOLVING SKILLS

CONFLICT RESOLUTION SKILLS

Just because we are trying to put ourselves in their shoes doesn't mean we are agreeing with them or 'caving'.

Once the other person feels heard, and if we feel we need to continue to address the matter, we can deliver another statement. This could be in the form of an 'I' statement if appropriate, but our language is always carefully chosen to remove any emotive content. What we are looking to do is to keep the conversation respectful while ensuring our message is heard and maintaining the integrity of the relationship.

Emma: *John, I'd like to talk to you about what happened in the meeting when you raised your voice, placed your pen down hard on the desk and walked quickly out of the room. It left everybody feeling unsettled, and I felt a little scared from what I saw.*

John: *I felt I had no choice. Nobody was listening to me and I got so frustrated.*

Emma: *You got angry because you felt you didn't have a voice in the meeting.*

John: *Yeah, that's right.*

Emma: *I think you'd agree there are other ways a situation like that can be handled, wouldn't you?*

John: *I know, I just got so mad. Nobody does anything around here. They're not pulling their weight and I'm sick of it.*

Emma: *It sounds like there are a couple of points here. Firstly, I'm glad you recognise there are alternatives, because that approach to dealing with frustration isn't what I expect from any of my team.*

John: *You're right. I'm sorry.*

Emma: *Thank you. Let's talk about the second point. You feel that the others aren't doing their fair share around here?*

Once John feels that he has been heard, I would suggest moving into a coaching conversation to explore other strategies John could employ when frustrated.

The conversational dance tends to lead to one of three outcomes:

1. John agrees congruently to solve the problem.
2. The conversation dissolves into a conflict of needs.
3. The conversation dissolves into a conflict of values.

Let's explore how we address the latter two scenarios.

CHAPTER 12

# Conflict Resolution Skills

*There are several strategies for dealing with conflict, and these are generally learned in childhood.*

Conflict in our personal and professional lives is unavoidable. Any time there is a shortage of resources or a difference of opinion, the stage is set for a potential conflict situation.

But that's a good thing, isn't it? In fact, it's a great thing! It's a great thing because a conflict situation gives us an opportunity to get creative and build an even stronger relationship with the other party or parties. There are generally two different types of conflict:

- Needs Conflict
- Values Conflict

Although both of them are conflict situations, how we deal with them is very different.

Figure 12-1

**Conflict Resolution Skills**

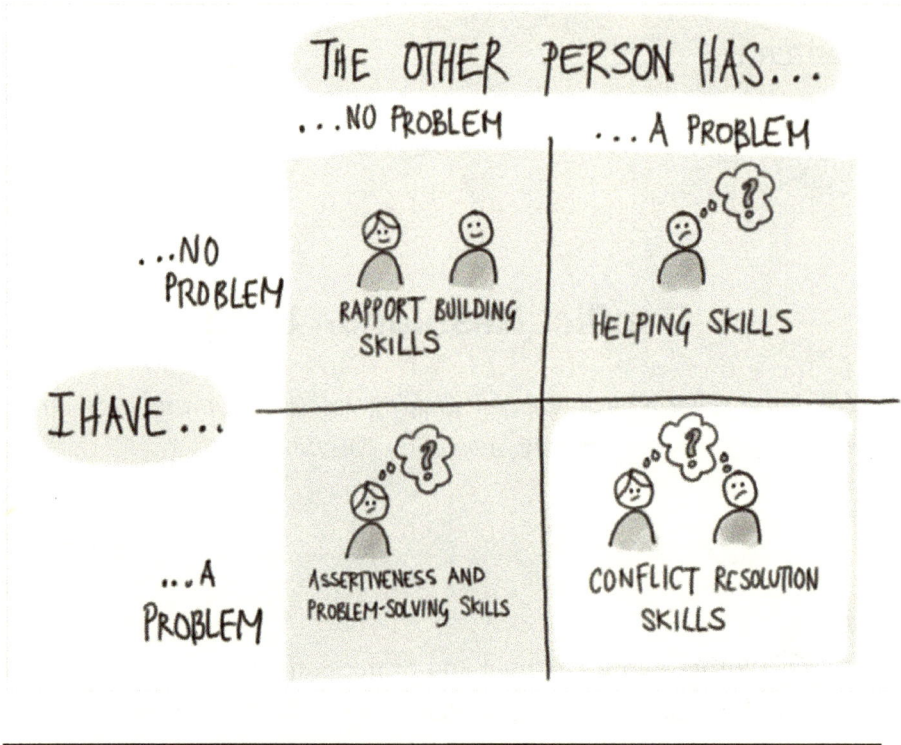

## Understanding the Needs Conflict

In his famous book *The 7 Habits of Highly Effective People*, Stephen Covey introduced the concept of win-win thinking. I always believed that every conflict situation needed to have a win-win. However, this is not always possible or even prudent. There are many ways to approach a conflict situation, the outcome of which comes down to how you view the importance of two things:

1. The relationship
2. The goal

Conflict is a common occurrence in families and relationships. Although traditionally viewed as negative, conflict approached in the right way can be a positive experience for the parties involved—with the correct orientation. There are several orientations people default to when engaging in conflict, and these orientations can directly impact the outcome of the disagreement.

People also have a learned tendency towards how they react when in a conflict situation, and this largely depends on the importance of their goal and the relationship between the parties. Because our strategies for dealing with conflict are learned, new and more effective strategies can also be learned.

Interpersonal conflicts can occur when the parties involved are in *I-You* or *I-Thou relationships,* and enter into a disagreement about how to arrive at an outcome. I-You and I-Thou relationships are among the three levels of communication distinguished by Julia Wood in *Interpersonal Communication.*

I-It communication is the first level. In this type of relationship, we treat other people impersonally and see them almost as objects. In I-You communication, the second level, we acknowledge one another but resist fully engaging with them. This level makes up for most of our interpersonal interactions.

Lastly, I-Thou relationships occur when individuals are open, see the other as important, and accept them for who they are, fully and completely. Therefore, although disagreements occur, because of the relationship it is important to the parties involved that the differences are resolved.

Although the traditional view believes that conflict is bad and should be avoided, contemporary view states that conflict can be useful in strengthening relationships. What's important is how the conflict is resolved. Positive conflict benefits the parties involved and can lead to better decisions and creative solutions to resolve the issue. Negative conflict is dysfunctional and impedes the ability to arrive at a mutually acceptable solution.

Conflict can be expressed overtly (open and explicit) or covertly (indirectly expressing feelings about disagreements). Overt conflict can occur through calm, measured conversation, although raised voices, arguments and physical violence are also demonstrations of overt conflict. Covert conflict occurs when a person deliberately attempts to upset or hurt another person through, for example, passive aggression (punishing a person without taking the blame for the action) or playing games (masking conflict behind excuses for arguing or criticising the other person).

## Approaches to Conflict

There are three basic ways of approaching conflict: lose-lose, win-lose, or win-win.

### Lose-Lose
The lose-lose approach to conflict assumes losses for all parties involved in the conflict and is detrimental and damaging to relationships.

### Win-Lose
Win-lose approaches to conflict, also known as distributive negotiations, determine that one party wins the conflict to the detriment of the other. Win-lose orientations are often found in cultures that value individualism and competition (for example, America), and are less common in cultures that value cooperation, such as Japan.

In some situations, a win-lose approach to conflict can undermine a relationship, because someone is on the losing end. However, win-lose situations may be appropriate when there is a high desire to win with little regard for the relationship, as in I-It relationships.

**Win-Win**

Win-win approaches to conflict, known as integrative negotiations, assume that both parties can benefit from a disagreement by working together to resolve it. This is generally only possible when the parties involved are dedicated to finding a mutually acceptable solution to the problem (a win-win). Working in collaboration towards a mutually acceptable solution often increases the respect between the parties involved and improves the relationship.

## Strategies for Dealing with a Needs Conflict

Our strategies for dealing with conflict are generally learned in childhood. As mentioned earlier, because these strategies have been learned, we can also learn new, more effective ways of dealing with conflict.

To reiterate: when engaging in conflict, there are two factors to be aware of—achieving an outcome that meets our goals and maintaining a relationship with the other person. Since the importance of attaining our goals and the importance of maintaining a relationship with the other party lie on separate continuums, Johnson and Johnson, in *Joining Together: Group Theory and Group Skills*, propose that there are five basic strategies to manage conflicts (see Figure 12-2):

1. Withdrawing
2. Forcing
3. Compromising
4. Smoothing
5. Confronting

***In conflict, be fair and generous.***
~ Lao Tzu

Figure 12-2

**Strategies for Dealing with a Needs Conflict**

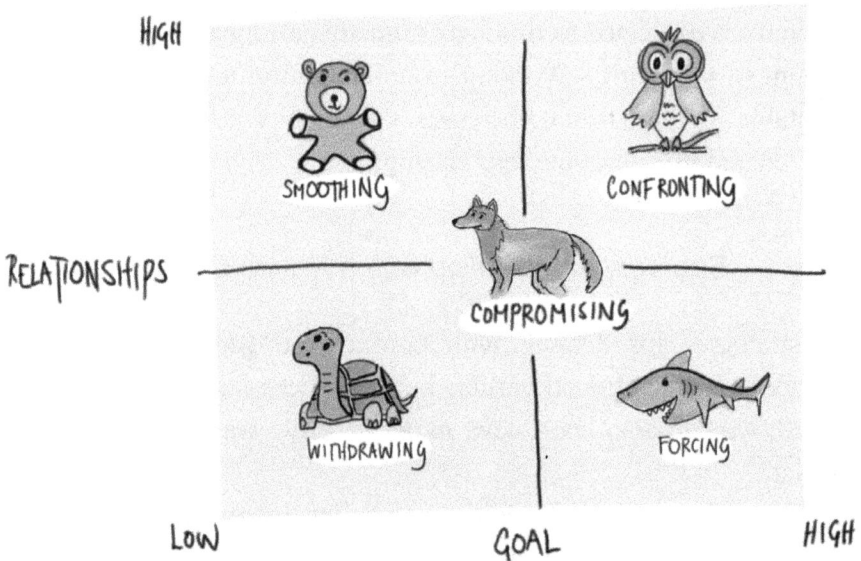

**Withdrawing**

Withdrawing, signified by the turtle, is recognised in people who avoid conflicts and withdraw into their metaphorical shell. This behaviour may occur when an individual doesn't value the goal and does not want to maintain a relationship with the other person: neither the goal nor the relationship is important.

This approach to dealing with conflict could be a good strategy in a situation where violence from the other party is likely.

**Forcing**

The second strategy, forcing (the shark), generally ends in win-lose outcomes. For the shark, the goal is very important and the relationship is not, so sharks tend to use tactics to persuade or force the other person to concede. These tactics may include making threats, imposing penalties and deadlines, or making demands beyond what is appropriate.

### Compromising

Compromising is characterised by the fox. The fox is only somewhat concerned with attaining the goal and maintaining the relationship. When neither party can get what they want, both parties give up a part of their desired outcome and sacrifice part of the relationship so that an agreement can be attained. Sometimes, parties who are both committed to a problem-solving approach (the fifth strategy) agree on a compromise because they are short on time.

### Smoothing

The fourth strategy is smoothing, represented by the teddy bear. To the teddy bear, the goal is of much less importance than the relationship. Maintaining a strong relationship is very important to the teddy bear, and they will often help the other person achieve their goal if they believe that person's interests are greater than their own.

### Confronting

The final strategy is the problem-solving approach, signified by the owl. To the owl, both the goal and the relationship are important, and the owl looks to initiate problem-solving negotiations to find a solution to the disagreement.

This is the best approach when both parties have a shared interest in the outcome or opposed interests in the outcome. In order for this approach to work, it is necessary for both parties to trust the other, be open, and reveal their underlying interests so that a mutually beneficial solution can be reached.

*Conflict cannot survive without your participation.*
~ Wayne Dyer

## *The Six-Step Formula*

There are six simple steps to maximise joint outcomes and lead toward a solution.

### Step 1 - Preparation and Defining the Problem

The first step encourages each party to communicate what they want in a non-evaluative and descriptive way. Only those parties involved in the conflict should be present. Encourage everyone to be involved in defining the problem. This is an important first step, because everyone has a right to express their interests and goals.

There are two key aspects to this step. The first is communicating using I-statements, and the second is demonstrating active listening, listening with interest, and paraphrasing. Being able to define the conflict as a shared problem tends to increase trust and improve communication and cooperation.

### Step 2 - Define the Problem in Terms of Needs

The next step is for each person to describe their needs and feelings. Needs and feelings should be expressed openly and should be recognised by the other party. This simple act deepens relationships and makes them more effective and personal. At this stage, don't accept sudden promises. Before moving on, double check that you have a mutually acceptable definition of all the needs and goals of all parties.

### Step 3 - Walk a Mile in the Other Person's Shoes

Step three is to exchange the reasons for each person's position on the disagreement. Whilst doing so, it is important to express cooperative intentions to finding a solution and to listen to the other person's reasons. Often by individuals revealing their underlying interests, a solution that works for both parties is made possible. Simply by putting ourselves in the shoes of others we can better understand their perspective, which changes our own self-interest towards a joint interest in resolving the conflict.

### Step 4 - Generate Alternative Solutions

During this step, we look to invent options for mutual gain. It consists of generating as many alternative solutions as possible (at least three!) before deciding on which one to move forward with. At this stage in the negotiation, it is important not to focus on a single answer to the problem and to remain open and flexible. The parties are encouraged to gather as much information as possible and get creative in searching for solutions that provide mutual gain. Every solution is written down.

### Step 5 - Evaluate the Solutions

Each solution is tested simply by asking, "Will it work?" Check to ensure it meets all of the needs and goals of each of the parties, and ask, "Are there any problems likely?" Continue to use active listening and 'I' statements.

### Step 6 - Choose and Implement the Solution

Step six is about reaching a wise agreement. A wise agreement is categorised as one that is fair to all parties. It is based on principles and lays the foundation for the resolution of future conflicts in a constructive manner.  Simply test for agreement and gain consensus. If agreement is difficult, summarise the areas in which everyone does agree, restate the needs of all parties, and look for new definitions of the problem that might offer more solutions.

Lastly, implement the solution and agree on who does what by when, etc. Refuse to remind or police the solution. It is important that each party commit to carrying out what was agreed.

In summary, when both parties are committed to attaining a mutually acceptable solution, then conflict can be a positive experience for the parties involved.

Although the most effective strategy for resolving conflict is the problem-solving approach (integrative negotiations), all strategies can be useful depending on the importance of the goal and the relationship.

An integrative approach using the basic six-step formula will often lead to beneficial outcomes for both parties.

Distributive negotiations tend to hinder positive outcomes when trying to resolve a conflict, and can also have a detrimental impact on the relationships between the parties.

## Understanding the Values Conflict

Several months ago, I was channel-surfing and I caught the end of a documentary about refugees flooding Europe from war-torn Syria. I joined the programme just as the reporter was traveling by car between two villages in Greece with his cameraman. It was in the middle of the day in the height of summer, with temperatures rising above forty degrees Celsius.

Along the dusty road they came across a woman dressed from head to toe in traditional Muslim garb, carrying a four-year-old child in one arm and a bag of belongings in the other. Her sandaled feet shuffled along in the dust, barely rising off the ground; she was clearly exhausted.

The next village was about forty kilometres away, so the reporter and the cameraman stopped and offered her a lift and some much-needed water. She guzzled down the water and was very appreciative of the help. Then she called ahead to let her brother and cousin know that she would be arriving soon.

Upon arrival, the brother and cousin came rushing out of the house and dragged her and the child out of the car, yelling and screaming at her. Without thanking the reporter and the cameraman, they turned and dragged the woman inside.

The reporter, not speaking the language, didn't understand a word that was said. The cameraman explained that they were chastising her for getting into a car with men she didn't know without their permission or without a male chaperon.

As they drove away, the reporter mused that providing housing, jobs and education will not be the biggest challenge when integrating people of different cultures. The biggest challenge will be integrating the value systems of these cultures.

A values conflict is much trickier to deal with than a needs conflict because, as we discussed earlier, values are unconscious beliefs about things that are important to us as people. Whenever two opposing values come into conflict, it can become deeply personal.

A values conflict need not be between two different cultures, but could come down to putting work over family or putting the welfare of others over making another dollar. So how do we address a values conflict? In his training programmes, Richard Bolstad lays out three approaches we can take to resolving a values conflict.

Remember, however, that although these approaches significantly increase the chance of resolving the conflict, there is never any guarantee when it comes to a values conflict.

### Utilising Shared Values

The first step in this approach is to identify the values that you and the other person share. Once you have this information, you can often address the conflict by developing solutions that work because they meet these shared values.

### Modelling

In order for you to model your values, you first must be sure of what these are and that your behaviour is an acceptable representation of these. If your relationship with the other person is healthy, and you really walk your talk, there is a good chance that the other person will change their behaviour and come to share your values. The impact of this skill is much greater than you might first anticipate. Remember, one way we develop our values is through the influence of significant others.

*Peace is not absence of conflict, it is the ability to handle conflict by peaceful means.*
~ Ronald Reagan

### Consulting

The consulting approach is a little more direct than the other two. It's referred to as the consulting approach because, just like in consulting, another person must be willing to hire you. In this instance, the other person must be willing to listen to you. The consulting process follows these simple steps:

1. Know the facts about your issue
2. Check that the other person is willing to listen to you (hire you)
3. Share your views respectfully, using 'I' statements
4. Listen to the other person's views using active listening
5. Leave the final decision to the other person, and do not hassle them
6. Continue to model your behaviour in line with your own values

Once again, the impact of this approach is easy to underestimate. Even though the other person might not necessarily agree with you at the time of the conversation, there is a strong chance they will change their value after some thought. By not following up and hassling them, it increases your ability to influence the change.

As you can see, it's vitally important to practice and implement these skills in the order in which they are presented here. Each skill builds on the other and further expands the likelihood of achieving the overall goal of expanding the 'No Problem' area in all of your relationships.

## Coach's Tip

There's a lot of great information here, and I'm often asked by my workshop participants, "Where do I start?" The best way to develop these skills is one week at a time. Take the skills in the first quadrant and practice them at every opportunity for the first week. Next, do the same for the second quadrant, and so on. The great thing about practicing these skills is that you won't be short of opportunities!

# CHAPTER 13

# Working Styles

*The advantage of this model is that it's not based on personality.*

I was running a workshop for coaches on anxiety some time ago, and one of the participants, a young guy, said something that completely stopped me in my tracks. He stated that everyone thinks the same, and therefore everyone thinks like he does.

I was dumbfounded, and at first thought I had misheard him. Before I could question him some more, everyone else in the room pounced on him and shared their opposite view! My point was made.

Although we are all unique in many ways, we do share some preferences for how we communicate and cope with certain situations. But we only share these preferences with approximately twenty-five percent of the population. In reality, three out of four people do these things differently than me:

- They think differently
- They decide differently
- They use time differently
- They handle their emotions differently

- They manage stress differently
- They communicate differently
- They deal with conflict differently (except, of course, until they read this book!)

I'm sure you've witnessed this yourself. People with significantly different behavioural patterns have a more difficult time building rapport with others, they are less likely to be influential with one another, they miscommunicate more often, and they tend to rub each other the wrong way just by being themselves!

Of course, when questioned about this, they respond, "It's just who I am, and you can't get on with everybody."

## The Dunedin Longitudinal Study

There are several models on communication, but they all tend to stem from the same research: the Dunedin Longitudinal Study. The longest-running research ever to be conducted on human development, this study has been recording the obstetric, perinatal and neonatal histories of more than 12,000 babies and their mothers since the mid-1970s. Every year of their lives, the participants undergo several tests, both psychological and physical, and some of the early findings have been ground-breaking.

Burton, Westen, and Kowalski highlight a few interesting findings in their book *Psychology: Australian and New Zealand Edition,* which is based around a trait that we all share called temperament. Although personality psychologists tend toward different models of how best to explain personality, there is one thing that they all agree on: Temperament is a personality trait that is with us from the moment we are born and changes very little as we age. It's spoken of as if it's in our DNA.

From the Dunedin Longitudinal Study, Burton, et al. state:

Those classified as 'difficult' at age three were more likely to have problems with alcohol or show a range of other antisocial behaviours as adults. Those who were classified as 'inhibited' at age three were much more likely to suffer from depression as adults (Silva & Stanton, 1996) (p. 438).

Burton, et al. go on:

While attachment style is predictive of later behaviour, temperament in early childhood is also remarkably stable in later life. An Australian longitudinal study by Lewis (1993) found that the temperament dimension of negative mood tone (anger and distress) at three months of age predicted poor cognitive performance at four years. In New Zealand, a longitudinal study of more than 800 boys and girls also revealed remarkable continuity in temperament (Caspi & Silva, 1995). Toddlers who were rough, easily distracted and prone to mood swings carried these traits into their teens. Those who lacked control at age three were likely to be risk takers or sensation seekers as they grew older. These data suggest children may have hereditary dispositions towards a certain temperament, but also tend to select an environment that matches (p. 500).

So what has all of this got to do with us? Well, temperament can be broken down into two sub-traits: assertiveness and emotional responsiveness. The model we'll be exploring next is based on the combination of these two traits.

## The Working Styles Model

Although many different models have been derived from the assertiveness and emotional responsiveness traits, the research by Dr David W. Merrill and expanded upon by Robert Bolton and Dorothy Grover Bolton in their book, *People Styles at Work... and Beyond,* is by far the best I've come across.

Having a basic understanding of the nature, uses, and limitations of the working styles model enables us to become more adept at improving our relationships. Models are simply tools of the mind, and they are designed to improve understanding and performance by reducing complexity to a manageable level. Understanding our working style is important, because it improves self-awareness and our understanding of ourselves, it shines a spotlight on the areas that might be leading to conflict with others, and it can lead to more harmonious and productive relationships.

The working styles model (see Figure 13-1) is so effective because it is based on clusters of a person's habitual assertive and emotionally responsive behaviours. These behaviours have a pervasive and enduring influence on our actions. The advantage of this model is that it's not based on personality, i.e. implicit values, characteristics, motives, attitudes, feelings, etc. It's based on explicit behaviour that can be seen and experienced in our day-to-day dealings with others.

For example, do you know anyone who is typically late for meetings? How about someone who tends to be very thorough? Have you ever met someone who keeps touching base with people? What about the person who has a story for nearly every occasion? Or do you know someone who is a no-nonsense, 'just do it' kind of person? Behavioural tendencies like these tend to remain fairly consistent from one situation to another, which makes it possible to predict how someone is likely to react in certain situations.

*There is an amazing power getting to know your inner self and learning how to use it and not fight with the world. If you know what makes you happy, your personality, interests and capabilities, just use them, and everything else flows beautifully.*
~ Juhi Chawla

Figure 13-1

**The Working Styles Model**

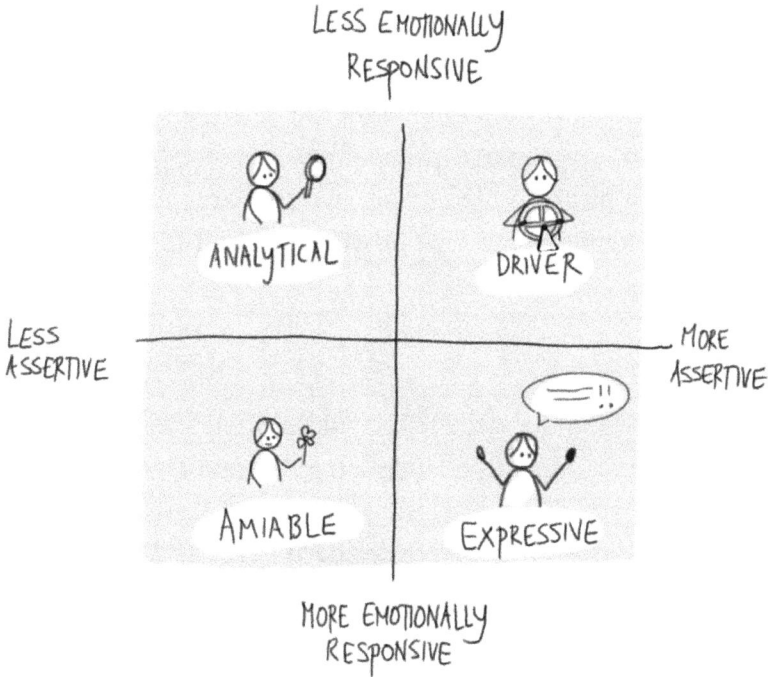

As we can see, from the combinations of assertiveness and emotional responsiveness, we get the following personas:
- DRIVER: More assertive, less emotionally responsive.
- EXPRESSIVE: More assertive, more emotionally responsive.
- AMIABLE: Less assertive, more emotionally responsive.
- ANALYTICAL: Less assertive, less emotionally responsive.

The names assigned to these are arbitrary. I've even seen models where colours and even animals are used.

The following descriptions are a summarised version of the great work Bolton and Bolton produced in their book.

**A Note on Flexing**

As we explore the different styles, we'll look at how to 'flex' to get a better outcome depending on which style you're communicating with. When flexing your preferred style to influence another person, it is important to temporarily adjust a few of your behaviours to make the exchange a little more comfortable for the other person. This will help to get them on the same wavelength before you take them in the direction you want to go. Remember, we are only flexing temporarily; we are not changing who we are or what we stand for.

## *Driver*

The Driver style is located in the upper-right area of the working styles grid. Drivers tend to be more assertive and less responsive than the average person. They are task-oriented and fast-paced. They tend to speak quickly, walk quickly, decide quickly and work quickly… and efficiently. They want and expect things done yesterday and they can sometimes even get impatient if the other person is not speaking, making decisions, and delivering at the pace they expect.

Drivers are all about delivery and getting things done. They have a sense of urgency about things, but the rushing into completing activities can sometimes cause less than desirable results; however, Drivers are just happy to be doing something.

Other theories reference the Driver style as Choleric (Hippocrates/Galen), Director (Jung), Action Man (Drucker), and Dominance (DISC).

*Always be yourself, express yourself, have faith in yourself, do not go out and look for a successful personality and duplicate it.*

~ Bruce Lee

Figure 13-2

**The Working Styles Model: Driver**

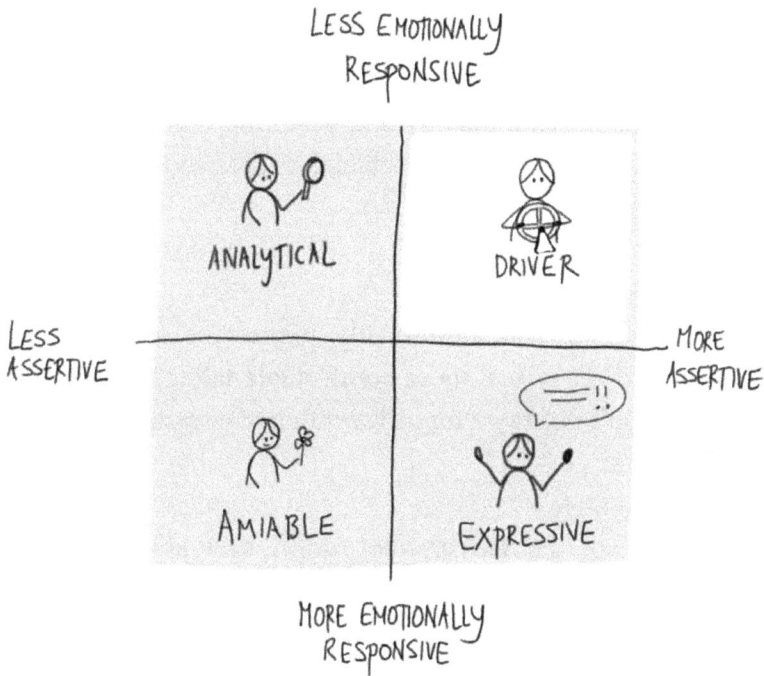

LESS EMOTIONALLY RESPONSIVE

ANALYTICAL

DRIVER

LESS ASSERTIVE

MORE ASSERTIVE

AMIABLE

EXPRESSIVE

MORE EMOTIONALLY RESPONSIVE

**Decision-Making**
Drivers are very decisive; they don't like leaving things open and will often make decisions without having all the relevant detail. They are certain about their views, but can change their minds when things aren't going to plan. Their desire for quick decision-making can sometimes lead to issues further down the track.

**Time Management**
If you want to see excellent time management in practice, watch a driver; this is where they excel. Drivers are very results-focused, and they like achieving tangible outcomes. They are great at setting clear

and measurable goals, and even better at setting out to achieve them. They enjoy their independence and like to set their own tasks.

### Body Language

Drivers are very definite in their body language. They stand tall and lean into things, moving quickly and gesturing quite forcefully. They use direct eye contact and their facial expressions come across as serious and tense.

### Relating to Others

Drivers are on the less emotionally expressive scale and can be difficult to read. They feel more comfortable talking about facts than feelings and don't portray a lot of warmth and empathy.

### Communication Style

True to nature of the Driver, they don't beat around the bush in expressing their opinions. They prefer to speak rather than email, but often use bullet points in written communication. Their communication is succinct and to the point, which can be viewed as rude or confrontational to others.

### Delivery Style

Drivers have a strong focus on the end result. They can be more focused on getting the project across the line than about the quality of the deliverable. Because they are more task-oriented, they tend to focus on the present and pay less attention to things that could go wrong down the track.

Drivers dislike small talk and can ignore other's feelings to achieve a task, but can also achieve a lot in a relatively short amount of time. When they are concerned about the well-being of others, they tend to demonstrate by action rather than through words, although this tends to go unnoticed. Ultimately, Drivers tend to be poor listeners and are much more interested in their opinion over that of others.

**Strengths**

Drivers are efficient, decisive, pragmatic, independent, and candid. These are all real strengths when it comes to getting things done. When Drivers overuse or misapply their strengths, they can come across as pushy, domineering and authoritarian. If in overdrive, they may push their forcefulness excessively, running roughshod over people's feelings and their turfs as they ramrod their ideas and objectives through. This may cause a drop in effectiveness as resentment and resistance in others grows.

Drivers need to be mindful of over-using their strengths. For example, because they thrive at independence, they can become poor collaborators. Their results-oriented approach can come across as being impersonal. When being candid, they can be perceived as being abrasive, and their pragmatism can be viewed as short-sightedness.

**Flexing to Analyticals**

Drivers and Analyticals tend to focus on tasks and have an objective approach to things. The biggest challenge for Drivers when dealing with Analyticals is to be mindful of their less assertive behaviour. Therefore, Drivers should focus on slowing their pace, listening more often, and listening attentively.

**Flexing to Amiables**

The Amiable is at the opposite end of the continuum, and therefore are the biggest communication challenge. To flex to an Amiable, Drivers need to focus on making genuine personal contact, slowing down, listening more often and attentively, providing a clear structure to work within, and being supportive when it is called for.

**Flexing to Expressives**

Both Drivers and Expressives share a love for getting things done and appreciate one another's energy. The challenge for the Driver is being aware of the Expressives' emotionally responsive side. A few things a Driver can focus on when flexing to an Expressive are to make personal contact, flex to the Expressives' spontaneity, and go with their fun-loving side. Expressives enjoy a lot of freedom and need a lot of praise… so give it to them!

### Flexing to Other Drivers

Two or more Drivers working together can lead to a strong focus on some things, but a complete lack of focus on others. It's important to consider the skills the other styles bring to the table; for example, focusing a little more on analysis before making a decision. Asking for the opinions of others, looking at the big picture, maintaining good stakeholder relationships, and keeping an eye on change management practices are all important considerations when Drivers find themselves working together.

## *Expressive*

The Expressive style is located in the lower-right area of the working styles grid. They are both higher in assertiveness and higher in responsiveness. Expressives like new shiny projects. Of all the styles, they are the most ostentatious. They love attention and love to receive lots of positive feedback. Expressives have a lot of energy and can influence the mood of a whole team. Their assertiveness and abundance of energy can be a bit too much for people at times. Expressives want to be in the middle of things and they naturally gravitate toward the fast-moving, exciting activities and always like to be on the move. Expressives are the most playful and fun-loving of all the styles, and being stuck in a chair for most of the day doesn't suit their style at all.

Other theories reference the Expressive style as Sanguine (Hippocrates/Galen), Intuitor (Jung), Front Man (Drucker), and Influencing (DISC).

Figure 13-3

**The Working Styles Model: Expressive**

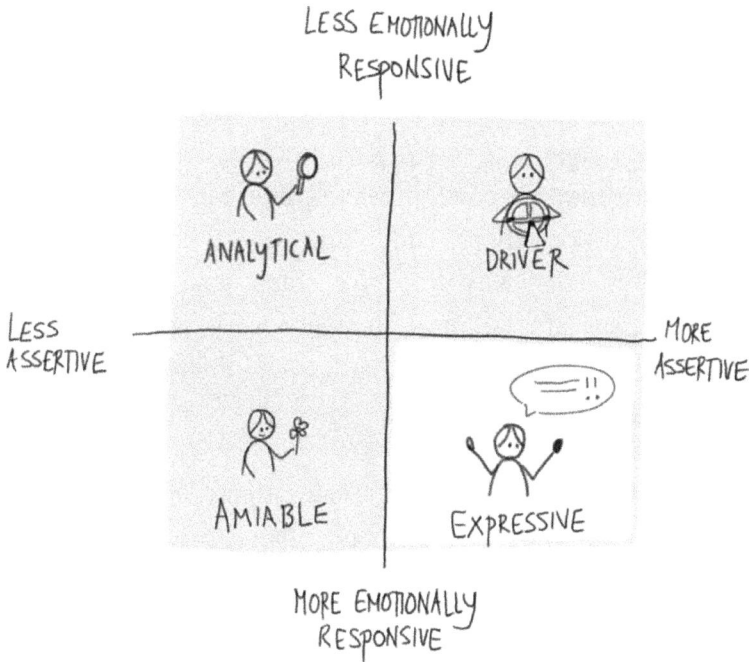

LESS EMOTIONALLY
RESPONSIVE

ANALYTICAL          DRIVER

LESS                                MORE
ASSERTIVE                          ASSERTIVE

AMIABLE            EXPRESSIVE

MORE EMOTIONALLY
RESPONSIVE

**Decision-Making**

Expressives are very impulsive and can change their minds on a dime (much to the frustration of Analyticals!). They tend to leap before they look and are emotionally driven decision-makers, often relying on gut instinct and intuition.

**Time Management**

Expressives are a disaster when it comes to time management. They are easily distracted by what's going on in the moment and end up being late for meetings and missing deadlines.

**Relating to Others**

With their outgoing personalities, Expressives relate well to others and tend to have a large circle of friends. Their natural energy can be motivating for people and they enjoy being in groups. Expressives are natural networkers.

**Communication Style**

Expressives are natural communicators and can be very persuasive. They are great storytellers, and often go off on tangents and use examples. They shy away from facts and tend to formulate their thoughts as they are talking. They are very animated with their gestures, talk rapidly, and make great use of intonation.

**Delivery Style**

Because Expressives are more people-oriented than task-oriented, they tend to get things done through other people. They don't like paperwork or wading through emails, and can get quite distracted during meetings unless the topic is relevant to them, whereupon they get involved in a very energetic way.

Expressives aren't good with detail and lack follow through. They tend to enjoy the sound of their own voice, and hence don't listen as much as they probably should, often interrupting others and dominating the conversation.

**Strengths**

Expressives are persuasive, enthusiastic, outgoing, spontaneous, and fun-loving. Spontaneity can be a double-edged sword, because overly spontaneous people can be difficult to work with. Not delivering on commitments due to being distracted by 'shiny things' in the moment can cause resentment and tension in others.

As with a Driver, an Expressive can overuse their strengths. For example, being overly articulate can lead to being a poor listener, being fast-paced can come across as being impatient, their skill as a visionary can be seen as impractical, and their fun-loving nature can be distracting.

### Flexing to Analyticals

Just like the Amiable is at the opposite end of the continuum from the Driver, the Analytical is at the opposite end of the continuum from the Expressive. Therefore, communicating with Analyticals is the Expressives' biggest challenge. When flexing to the Analytical, the Expressive should slow their pace, listen more often and attentively, focus on the task, be organised, factual and systematic, and reduce the emphasis on feelings.

### Flexing to Amiables

Expressives and Amiables both understand the importance of relationships. To get in synch with an Amiable's less assertive behaviours, Expressives should slow down, be supportive when necessary, and, yes, listen more often and listen attentively.

### Flexing to Drivers

When dealing with Drivers, Expressives need to be mindful of being more task-oriented, reduce the emphasise on feelings, be well organised and have a plan. Also, be mindful of any potential power struggles that may arise.

### Flexing to Other Expressives

As with Drivers, when Expressives are working together, there are certain things they need to focus on. For example, they need to become more serious and pay attention to the details. Taking a more systematic approach and using more negotiation will promote a better outcome.

## *Amiable*

The Amiable style is located in the lower-left area of the working styles grid. Amiables demonstrate less assertiveness but higher responsiveness than the average person. They have a strong people-orientation and an easy-going, friendly manner that brings a certain warmth and harmony to their exchanges with other people; this, of course, is a huge asset when it comes to working with others. Amiables have a strong empathy; they are very much in touch with their own emotions and quite easily pick up on the emotions of others. They are concerned about what other people think and want, and they are more open to hearing others' thoughts and ideas than in voicing

Figure 13-4

**The Working Styles Model: Amiable**

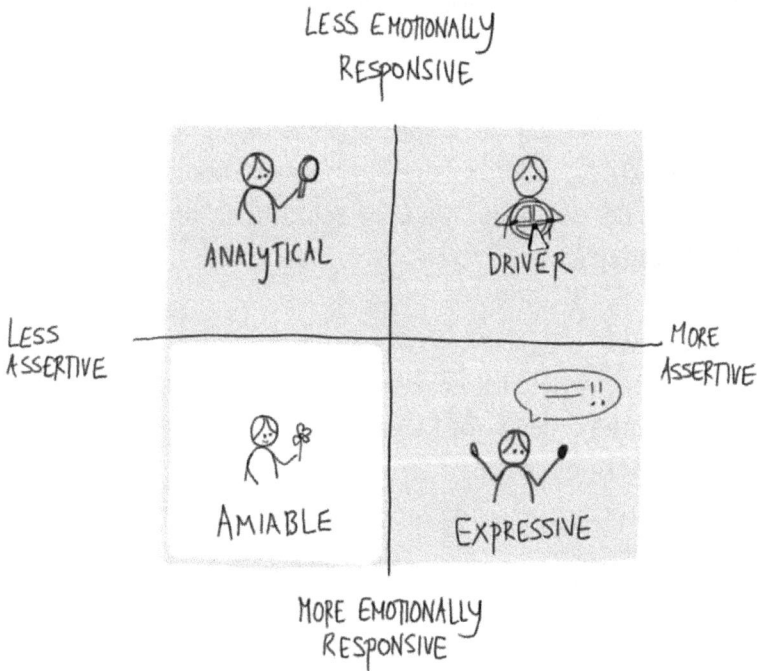

their own. Because of this, people often seek them out as confidantes.

Due to their personable nature, the Amiable enjoys working in small groups or, especially, one-on-one. They don't seek out the limelight and avoid ego clashes. They often encourage others to develop their ideas and are adroit at uncovering the value in other people's contributions that might be otherwise discounted by others. They are often effective at bringing together divergent opinions into a solution that everyone involved can genuinely support and get behind. Amiables are very good team players and give freely of their time, often volunteering to undertake the grunt work of the team.

Other theories reference the Amiable style as Phlegmatic (Hippocrates/Galen), Feeler (Jung), People Man (Drucker), and Steadiness (DISC).

### Decision-Making
Amiables tend to be cautious about making decisions; they like guarantees and tend to avoid risk. They are very collaborative in their decision-making and often consult others in the process.

### Body Language
Relaxed and low-key, Amiables tend to be slower paced than the other styles. They lean back in a chair when making a request and their voice is warm and low. As you might imagine, they are comfortable with eye contact and are facially expressive.

### Relating to Others
Amiables build strong empathetic relationships. They are open about their feelings but tend to suppress unresourceful emotions, such as anger. Amiables are uncomfortable with conflict and avoid confronting others about a problem, preferring to complain to a third party. They are tactile by nature and are very attuned to the feelings of others. Amiables are slow to anger (but can be slow to forgive if pushed too much!) and enjoy harmonious environments.

## Communication Style

Quiet by nature, Amiables are quieter than others and tend to be slower to form opinions (sometimes too late in the piece). They are genuinely interested in other people and are attuned to the impact changes to the environment might have on them; they focus more on the human side of business. Amiables are less likely to speak up and will often withhold their point of view if divided on an opinion.

## Delivery Style

Amiables like to work within a stable environment with a clear structure. They prefer to have goals set for them and follow direction well. Amiables are industrious workers and are very service-oriented. They enjoy the day-to-day routine and quietly get through their work.

Because Amiables have less of a focus on task, they can sometimes miss deadlines or fail to deliver in a timely fashion. They often bend to the will of others rather than upset the apple cart, and they state opinions indirectly, preferring to make a request rather than saying what's really on their minds.

## Strengths

The Amiable is a great team player. They are cooperative, supportive, diplomatic, patient, and loyal. Amiables work harmoniously with others, however they also have a propensity to avoid conflict and sweep unpleasant facts under the rug. This may cause doubt in others in controversial situations.

An Amiable's strength as a diplomat may be perceived as a conflict avoider. Being overly cautious can come across as being risk-averse, being too supportive can be interpreted as being permissive, and being too people-oriented can be perceived as being inattentive to the task at hand.

## Flexing to Analyticals

Being less assertive than the other styles, Amiables and Analyticals appreciate each other's low-key ways. The major challenge for

Amiables with Analyticals is to get in sync with their less responsive behaviours. Therefore, they need to be more task-oriented, focus less on feelings, be more systematic, and be better organised, detailed, and factual in their approach.

### Flexing to Drivers

As mentioned previously, Drivers and Amiables are at opposite ends of the continuum, so flexing to a Driver is the Amiable's biggest communication challenge. They need to pick up their pace and demonstrate higher energy. They should focus more on the task and be clear about their plan of action, be articulate and get to the point.

### Flexing to Expressives

Amiables and Expressives both understand the importance of relationships, but to better influence an Expressive, an Amiable needs to demonstrate more energy, pick up their pace, focus on the big picture, say what's on their mind, and act with determination.

### Flexing to Other Amiables

To facilitate the strengths of the other styles, Amiables working together should be more time-conscious and goal-oriented, assert a different point of view if needed, spend less time on interpersonal issues, and be mindful of coming up with insipid thoughts to avoid rocking the boat.

## *Analytical*

The Analytical style is located in the upper-left area of the working styles grid. Analyticals have a less than average assertiveness with a less than average responsiveness. They strongly value perfectionism and prefer exactness and quality over quantity. They like to ensure that the things they are associated with are correct. They

Figure 13-5

**The Working Styles Model: Analytical**

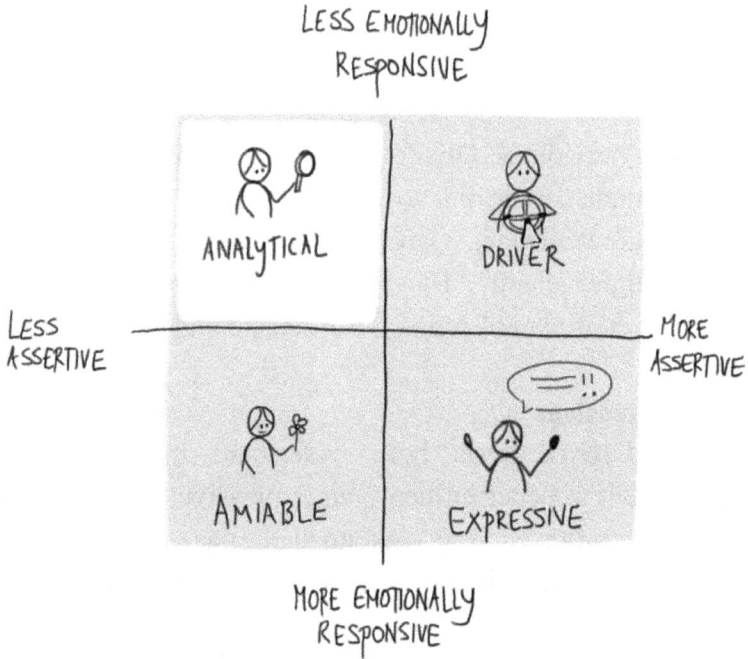

have very high standards for themselves and put the work in to achieve or even exceed these standards. Analyticals relish detail and

believe even the smallest feature of a project, no matter how irrelevant, adds to a quality outcome. They tend to be uncomfortable with quick fixes and like to ensure the solution is robust and well thought through.

Other theories reference the Analytical style as Melancholic (Hippocrates/Galen), Thinker (Jung), Thought Man (Drucker), and Compliance (DISC).

### Decision-Making

Analyticals are cautious when facing risks and they like to take their time when making a decision. Being right is important to the Analytical. They are very thorough and don't like making a recommendation unless they have all the facts!

### Time Management

Oddly enough, Analyticals tend to be on time for meetings, but can miss delivery deadlines. This is because of their strong desire to get things right—they hold themselves, and others, to very high standards. They deliver high-quality work, but often get tripped up by time constraints, leaving things unfinished or becoming a bottleneck.

### Body Language

Similar to the Amiable, Analyticals are pretty low-key with their body language. They don't gesture very much, lean back in their chair when making a point, avoid eye contact as a rule, and show less facial expressiveness. Because they don't talk about feelings and stick to the facts, they can come across as cold and can sometimes be difficult to read.

### Relating to Others

Analyticals are reserved by nature, and many would be the archetypical introvert. They give off an air of aloofness, as if they would prefer a good book to a party. Analyticals have a deep sense of fairness and can be very loyal when the chips are down. During conflict they become detached and rational, which can often frustrate the other styles.

### Communication Style

Generally quiet by nature, Analyticals speak less than other people unless they are diving into the details about something that interests them. They have a slower pace conversational style, with very little intonation or inflection in their voice. They like to think things through before saying anything, and are often continuing to think even when speaking. At odds with the Driver, Analyticals prefer the written word over talking, and structure their thoughts logically. Similar to the Amiable, they are more likely to make a request than state their opinion directly.

### Delivery Style

Analyticals love data! The more the better, although this can be their downfall because they can get bogged down in the detail and be slow to respond. They are very well organised and go about their work in a systematic fashion. They are terrific at building valuable processes, and the quality of their work is second to none. Unfortunately, Analyticals can fall into a by-the-book mindset, which is frustrating for other styles.

Most Analyticals are perfectionists by nature and can be pretty hard on themselves (and others!). They are slow to give positive feedback but quick to criticise, and they rarely give out compliments.

### Strengths

Analyticals are logical, systematic, thorough, prudent, and serious. If the Analytical's quest for quality degenerates into perfectionism, this particular strength becomes a liability. It is this trait that, when taken to the extreme, can often lead to failing to meet project deadlines.

### Flexing to Amiables

Analyticals and Amiables both enjoy the laid back and less assertive nature of the other, but Analyticals need to become more aware of the Amiables' more responsive behaviours. To do this, they should look for opportunities to make genuine personal contact, focus on feelings, and be supportive. Providing structure for Amiables is important, and holding back on the facts and focusing on the human side of things will win Amiables over.

### Flexing to Drivers

Analyticals and Drivers share a practical nature—none of this fluffy emotional stuff! However, for an Analytical to get on board with a Driver, they need to pick up the pace with an eye on delivery, act more energetically, and speak up with a results-focused mindset. Don't unnecessarily dive into the details and theory; if a Driver needs this information, they'll ask for it.

### Flexing to Expressives

Being at the opposite end of the continuum, Expressives are the Analyticals' biggest communication challenge. They need to focus on acting more energetically and working at pace. Personal contact is important to Expressives, and therefore the Analytical should focus more on feelings. Giving them loads of praise and being open to their fun side or spontaneity will go a long way toward winning an Expressive over. Lastly, Expressives love freedom, so make sure they have it in spades!

### Flexing to Other Analyticals

As for the other styles, when Analyticals work together, there are a few things they need to be mindful of. Firstly, they need to be more decisive and challenge each other on the level of detail they might dive into. Keeping an eye on the bigger picture is useful for Analyticals, and being open to other people's opinions is important. Lastly, recognising the human side of things is always valuable, as is maintaining strong relationships with others.

## How Stress Influences a Person's Style

We all default to a different way of responding to things when we are overloaded with stress. This often results in inappropriate behaviour that can be extreme and leads to inflexibility. Functioning under stress detracts from a person's effectiveness and has a detrimental impact on relationships. People's words and actions can be inappropriate when they are under stress, and their behaviour can be unfitting for the situation or the environment, often causing upset in others. A normally adaptable person may become inflexible in the extreme, regardless of the damage this approach might cause to their reputation or relationships.

## *Acute Stress*

When under acute stress, each style has a certain way of working.

Table 13-1

**Styles Under Acute Stress**

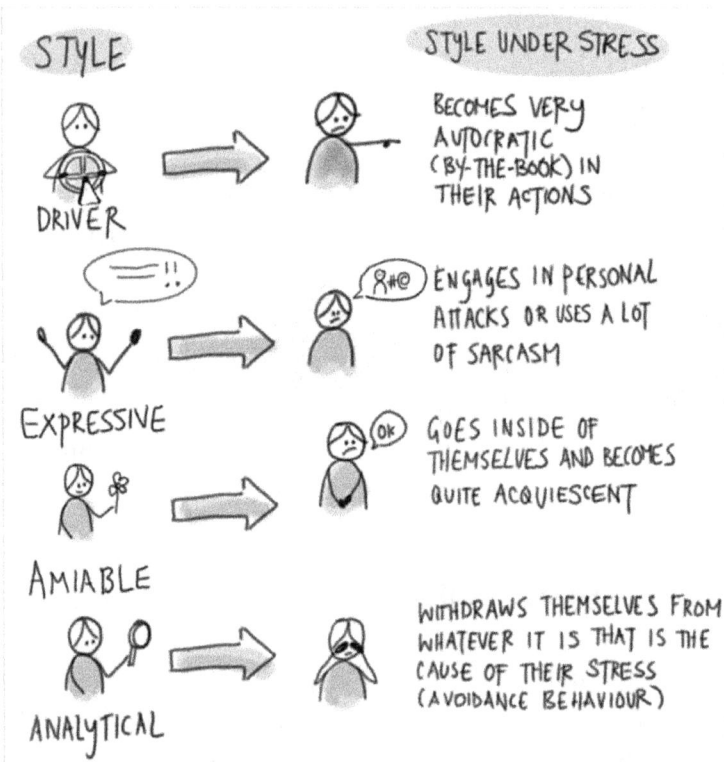

## *Chronic Stress*

After people shift into their default coping style, their tension dissipates and they return to their normal behaviour. But occasionally, the stress continues to build, and the person is catapulted into their secondary coping style. This generally consists of people moving to the opposite end of the assertion scale (see Figure 13-6).

- A Driver adopting an autocratic style will take on avoiding tendencies.
- An Expressive adopting an attacking style will take on acquiescing tendencies.
- An Amiable adopting an acquiescing style will take on attacking tendencies.
- An Analytical adopting an avoiding style will take on autocratic tendencies.

Figure 13-6

**Styles Under Chronic Stress**

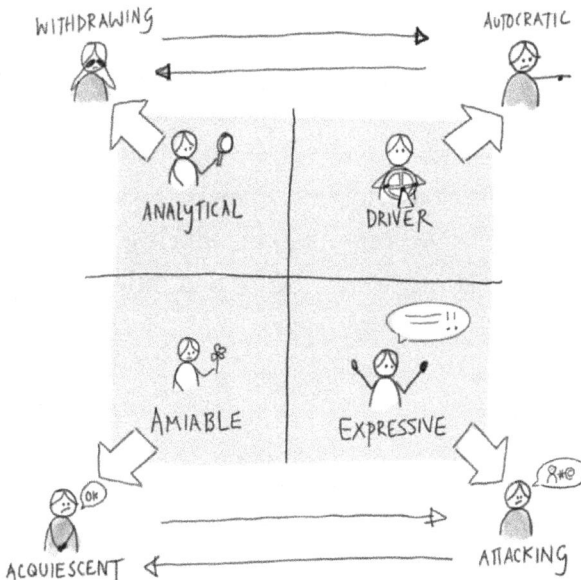

## *Determining a Person's Style with Two Simple Questions*

Now that you have an in-depth view of each of the styles, I'd like to share with you a very simple formula for determining a person's preferred working style. This is done by asking yourself two simple questions about the other person.

1. Is this person more assertive or less assertive than fifty percent of the people I know?

If the answer is more assertive, then they are either going to be a Driver or an Expressive. Less assertive would be Analytical or Amiable. We've already narrowed down the field!

2. Is this person more emotionally responsive or less emotionally responsive than fifty percent of the people I know?

If the answer is more emotionally responsive, then they are going to be either an Amiable or an Expressive, otherwise they will be an Analytical or a Driver.

Put the two answers together, and you get the person's preferred working style. This is a great place to start. From here, start to look for behaviours that either prove or disprove your hypothesis. Become a Working Styles Sherlock Holmes. Eventually, you'll be able to determine a person's style very quickly, which will naturally improve your ability to build strong relationships and influence others.

# Conclusion

*You don't hire the hand, you hire the person[2].*

I opened the introduction by stating that I wrote this book for a much younger me. These are all the things I wish I had known when I started my journey.

I think it was Peter Drucker who said, "You don't hire the hand, you hire the person[2]." Apart from the obvious gender reference, I couldn't agree more. It's not possible to leave who you are at the doors to your office. All the stresses and challenges we face in life come with us. The tools and strategies in this book will help you as much in your personal life as they will in your professional life.

But there is a truth that I haven't shared with you yet, and this truth will make all the difference.

I leave you with one wish. Don't just put this book back on the shelf. Do the exercises and put into practice what you've learned. It's only through taking deliberate action, failing, learning, practicing, and

---

[2] The original quote from Drucker is "You don't hire the hand, you hire the man", however, I'm more comfortable with this interpretation.

taking more action that you will grow and shape the leader within you.

Remember, you are fully capable of leading others, but first, you must lead yourself.

Lastly, for those of you who have read this book and passed it onto someone you believe it will be of benefit to, thank you. I believe that the little changes we make in ourselves can't help but make little changes in others… and together, we can create a better world.

Lead with purpose.

*I am not afraid of an army of lions led by a sheep; I am afraid of an army of sheep led by a lion.*
~ Alexander the Great

## Author's Note

*In the beginning, they creeped me out, but now I was numb to even the thought of them crawling over me when I slept.*

When I set out to write this book, the question "Who am I writing this book for?" kept going around and around in my mind until the answer popped up.

I'm writing this book for me... a much younger me. A *me* who found himself on the other side of the world renting a room "that would suit a gentleman." I quickly realised that no woman would ever stay there. It was a large house in Burwood, Western Sydney, with separate rooms for each resident, and it was a place where dreams go to die. I was broke and I was miserable.

One morning I found myself lying on the lumpy mattress watching my roommates—cockroaches—scurrying around the floor, up the walls, and across the ceiling. In the beginning, they creeped me out, but now I was numb to even the thought of them crawling over me when I slept. The sun battled to break through the grime on the window and a television set blared from a neighbouring room.

"Imagine having all your belongings and living your life in one room," I thought.

I was on my first big trip away from home, backpacking around the world. I had already taken in Bangkok, travelled through Malaysia on a thirty-six-hour bus trip, and spent some time in Singapore. The plan was to spend most of the year working in Australia, save up some money, and then travel around Australia, New Zealand and the United States.

I wasn't quite sure how I was going to do that on $200… which was all I had left.

A week earlier, I had been out knocking on doors, selling restaurant vouchers that offered two-for-one meals. I was hungry and tired, but I was also desperate, so I kept going. I was just approaching yet another house when a guy in his early thirties pulled up in a red Porsche 911. As he walked up the driveway, I saw he was tall, well-dressed, and moved with an air of confidence.

I thought to myself, "I'm going to sell to this guy!"

I gave him my pitch and he listened patiently. Then he said, "I liked your pitch, but I'm not going to buy from you today. I really admire the work you do, because door-to-door selling is hard. It's really hard. I don't sell door-to-door, but I sell insurance over the phone."

He looked back at his Porsche and said, "And the commission is pretty good. If ever you want to sell insurance, let me know."

He handed me his business card. I was sold! His name is David Hassib, and he took me under his wing for a short time—but that was all I needed.

I met with David a couple of times, and a few days later, I climbed off my bed, rummaged around in my bag, and pulled out the cassette tape David had loaned to me. I'd never listened to an audio book before, but I needed something to drown out the noise of the TV; it was driving me crazy!

I'll never forget the first words of that tape quoting Helen Keller:

"Life is either a daring adventure or nothing."

The next voice that I heard was that of Anthony Robbins, telling me that there is power in making a decision. I was in such a low place, I figured I had nothing to lose, and so that's exactly what I did. I made the decision that I wouldn't be going home with my tail between my legs, and proceeded to find a job and move into more suitable accommodation.

I set big goals, and I started to achieve them all! When I got back to Ireland after travelling around for the year, I worked three jobs while studying Physical Therapy. To say I was exhausted was an understatement, but there was no talking to me, I was focussed like never before. After a few years, I decided I wanted to move into Information Technology, so I got a job in a startup technology firm in Dublin and they paid for my degree.

After a few years, my wife and I moved to New Zealand, and although I continued to work hard, I hit a plateau in my life. I felt my career had stalled and I wasn't happy.

It was around that time that I met a wonderful Irish lady named Moira Mallon. Moira and I would catch up for a coffee from time to time, and I eventually shared with her some of the frustrations I was having. Moira had an amazing ability to ask the right questions or to phrase things in such a way that made sense. Little did I know I was getting top-of-the-line coaching, all for the price of a cup of coffee!

Moira was the first leadership coach I had ever met. I had never realized it was an actual profession, and she was very good at it. Moira continued to help me home into what it was that I would love to do, and working with people and helping them grow kept coming up. My interest in human performance and leadership started to reignite, and I threw myself into research, signed up for a two-year leadership coach training course, and went back to university to study psychology.

My hunger and drive was insatiable (as it is even to this day!). I quit my job, but still there was a growing fear that had the potential to derail my ambitions. I shared with Moira that "no one knows me as a leadership coach. I don't think I have the credibility to succeed."

She looked directly in my eyes and said, "Cillín, it's your passion that will get you through."

I held onto those words like a lifeline, and she was right. After months and months of toil, rejections and lessons, eventually things started to take hold. I no longer felt like a fraud. I was making a big difference in the lives of the people I worked with. The feedback they shared touched me in ways I could never have imagined.

This book is the one book I wish I'd had available to me when I was lying on that lumpy mattress in Burwood. The lessons and exercises in this book will help you grow into the person you want to be, create the life you want for yourself, and become a leader people want to follow.

RESULTS COACHING
EXPAND YOUR HORIZONS

**Results Coaching exists for one purpose**, to help you achieve your goals in life and get the results you deserve. Regardless of where you are in your life or your career, we'll help get you to where you want to be. Through one-on-one coaching and leadership development programmes we've had the privilege of working with some amazing people from some of New Zealand's most iconic companies.

We're less interested in showing up for a day and delivering a great training programme but focus more on achieving a tangible outcome for the organisation. We achieve this through ensuring that all of our programmes have a long 'tail' to them so that the material becomes practiced and embedded so the results are evident.

Here are some of the programmes we've designed and delivered to some of our valued customers:

- Values & Behaviours
- Resilience
- Working Styles Profile
- Developing Trust
- Growth Mindset

- Advanced Communication
- Coaching for Leaders
- Team Vision & Execution Plan
- Higher Productivity
- From Manager to Leader

The early years of a person's life are arguably the most important. Every year, the Neonatal Trust does outstanding work to give children and families the help they need for the best possible start under challenging circumstances.

That's why we're proud to support The Neonatal Trust by donating 10% of all profits generated from the sale of this book.

Every 90 minutes in New Zealand, a baby is born that requires specialist care. That's 5,000 babies EVERY YEAR.

The Neonatal Trust exists to support families going through the stress and anxiety of a neonatal journey, and to support the enhanced care of their precious premature and/or sick full-term babies.

The three core objectives of The Neonatal Trust are to:
- Support neonatal families through the stress and anxiety of their journey
- Fund neonatal research to increase understanding and enhance outcomes
- Support neonatal units and their staff so the babies receive the best care possible

As an insight into the stress and anxiety that can be involved with neonatal journeys . . .

*"I held her for the first time when she was two weeks old. She weighed less than 500 grams at that point and was in pretty bad shape. It was a scary experience, but very special. Once her condition became more stable, her Dad and I would take turns giving her kangaroo (skin to skin) cuddles each day."*

Charlotte's Mum
Charlotte was born at 23 weeks and 3 days gestation (16 weeks early)

To learn more, head to www.neonataltrust.org.nz.

# Acknowledgements

When I started writing this book, I had every intention of finishing it in two weeks. It made perfect sense. I knew what I wanted to say and how to say it… or so I thought. Nine months later and I find myself still writing the final words.

In reality, this book has been in the making for the last eight years, and as I look back on that journey, there are so many people who have contributed. The amount of people to thank will always be too much to capture in a few pages, so for those I haven't mentioned, please accept my apologies and my heartfelt thanks.

There would be no journey without my parents, Ann and Liam Hearns. Thank you for the freedom to choose and for supporting me in my decisions, even when they weren't the right ones. I often reflect on the headaches I caused you now that I am a father, and I admire how you navigated those rocky shores.

I am blessed to have two brothers and two sisters, all of whom have been an inspiration to me.

To Liam, my older brother, you gave me the courage to leave the shores of Ireland, explore the world, and expect more from life.

My younger sisters, Sinéad and Aisling, are two of the strongest women I know. Both are hugely successful in their chosen fields and care deeply about family and friends. They are two beautiful souls I am proud to know.

Lastly, my younger brother, Eamonn. Eamonn has always followed his heart and is one of the most value-driven people I have ever met. I feel honoured to be his brother. Eamonn is the kind of guy that everyone wants to be their best friend, and I am one of only four who can call him a brother.

As I mentioned in the introduction, my journey really started by the chance encounter with a man named David Hasib. I only knew David for a few short weeks, but his kindness and generosity has had a direct influence on my life, even over twenty years later.

I wouldn't be able to complete my thanks without including the early coaches in my life, Leanne Babcock, Michelle Dalley, and Mal Winnie. Thank you for helping me get started on my coaching journey.

There were two people who came along at a pivotal time in my life who need special mention: Dr David Keane and Moira Mallon, two Irish expats living in New Zealand. I attended David's 'The Art of Deliberate Success' programme, and it was my first exposure to a personal development programme. David was extremely generous with not only his time and his advice, but also his encouragement and belief that I could achieve my dream.

Soon after meeting David, Moira came into my life and helped me shape my future plans through her sage questioning and endless encouragement.

I remember when I quit my job and started coaching. I was hugely excited, but quickly realised that not many people knew me as a coach, and people weren't exactly beating down my door. Therefore, a huge thanks must go to Natasha Steadman, my first client. Thank you for giving me the opportunity and for putting your faith in me to be your coach. It means more to me than you will ever know.

There were a lean few months, but slowly things start to take off, and the people who made this possible are Blair Loveday, Claire O'Rourke, Sarah Gibson, Grant Robinson, Justine Carrington, Noel Dykes, and Simon Anderson.

Anything in life I'm passionate about, I throw myself into with gusto. Leadership and coaching are no different, and I have been studying everything I could get my hands on. Two people who have been influential in my studies are Richard Bolstad and Yulia Kurusheva. Both are amazing trainers, coaches and authors, and have really opened my eyes to creating therapeutic change through Neuro Linguistic Programming. Not only are they both experts in their field, they are two of the most genuine, warm-hearted people you will ever meet. Thank you both for awakening in me the passion for a subject that will keep my nose in a book for the rest of my life.

I would like to thank all of my clients who I have had the privilege of working with over the years. I can think of no greater reward than being trusted to walk alongside you into the most vulnerable areas of life and be part of a life-changing breakthrough. I have grown so much as a person, and often feel that I have learned more from you than I could ever offer you. Thank you for trusting me to be your coach, I am humbled by your strength and courage. It has been an honour.

I would also like to thank my illustrator, Kim Quirke, for the amazing illustrations throughout the book that really capture the meaning I have tried to portray through words. And thanks need to go to my editor, Calee Allen, for her keen eye, insightful suggestions, and her endless patience in crafting the final work. Any mistakes in the writing are mine and mine alone.

I have saved this last acknowledgement for a very special person in my life, my beautiful and long-suffering wife, Louise. You have been such a strong influence in my life, it's difficult to put into words. Your support and your belief in me gave me the courage to start on this journey, and it is only your endless sacrifices and infinite patience that has made the writing of this book possible. The words that I shared on our wedding day still ring true, even to this day.

*You are my rock when I need support,*
*My clown when I need to laugh,*
*My Zen garden when I need peace,*
*And my boot when I need a kick in the arse.*

Thank you. I love you.

# Bibliography

*We are like dwarfs sitting on the shoulders of giants. We see more, and things that are more distant, than they did, not because our sight is superior or because we are taller than they, but because they raise us up, and by their great stature add to ours.*
**– John of Salisbury**

Adler, R. B., Rosenfeld, L. B., & Proctor, R. F., II (2007). *Interplay: The process of interpersonal communication* (10th ed.). New York, NY: Oxford University Press.

Bolstad, R. (2016). *Transformations NLP master practitioner certification manual: Mastering success and mastering transformation.* Transformations International Consulting & Training Ltd.

Bolon, R., & Bolton, D. G. (2009). *People styles at work...and beyond: Making bad relationships good and good relationships better* (2nd ed.). NY, Amacom.

Brannon, L., & Feist, J. (2010). *Health psychology: An introduction to behaviour and health* (7th ed.). Belmont, CA: Wadsworth Cengage Learning.

Burton, L., Westen, D., & Kowalski, R. (2009). *Psychology* (2nd Australian & New Zealand ed.). Milton, Australia: Wiley.

Cervone, D., & Pervin, L. A. (2013). *Personality: Theory and research* (12th ed.). Hoboken, NJ: Wiley.

Day, S. X. (2008). *Theory and design in counselling and psychotherapy* (2nd ed.). Belmont, CA: Brooks/Cole.

De Janasz, S. C., Dowd, K. O., & Schneider, B. Z. (2012). *Interpersonal skills in organisations* (4th ed.). New York, NY: McGraw-Hill Irwin.

Dilts, R. (1999). *Sleight of mouth: The magic of conversational belief change*. U.S.A, Meta Publications.

Dilts, R. (2003). *From coach to awakener*. U.S.A, Meta Publications.

Duckworth, A (2016). *Grit: The power of passion and perseverance*. London, Vermilion.

Geldard, D., & Geldard, K. (2009). *Basic personal counselling: A training manual for counsellors* (6th ed.). Frenchs Forest, NSW, Australia: Pearson Education, Australia.

Grinder, J., & Bandler, R. (1976). *The structure of magic II: A book about communication and change*. California, SBB.

Johnson, D. W., & Johnson, F. P. (2013). *Joining together: Group theory and group skills* (11th ed.). Boston, MA: Pearson.

Kunert, M. (2009). *Pathophysiology: Concepts of altered health states* (8th ed., pp. 198-213). Philadelphia, MA: Lippincott Williams & Wilkins.

Madanes, C. (2010). *Relationship breakthrough: How to create outstanding relationships in every area of your life*. London, UK: Macmillan Publishers Limited.

Morris, C. G., & Maisto, A. A. (2005). *Psychology: An introduction* (12th ed.). Upper Saddle River, NJ: Pearson Education.

Myss, C. (2003). *Sacred contracts: Awakening your divine potential.* New York, NY: Harmony Books.

Neill, M. (2006). *Supercoach. 10 secrets to transform anyone's life.* Alexandria, NSW. Hay House Australia Ltd.

Nelson-Jones, R. (1993). *Practical counselling and helping skills: How to use the lifeskills helping model* (3rd ed.) London, UK. Cassell Educational Limited.

Lencioni, P. (2002). *The five dysfunctions of a team: A leadership fable.* San Francisco: Jossey-Bass.

Robbins, A. (1992). *Awaken the giant within: How to take immediate control of your mental, emotional, physical and financial destiny!* New York, NY: Summit Books.

Santrock, J. W. (2012). *Essentials of life-span development* (2nd ed.). New York, NY: McGraw-Hill.

Schafer, W. (2000). *Stress management for wellness* (4th ed.). Belmont, CA: Wadsworth Group/Thomson Learning.

Schucman, H. (2007). *A course in miracles* (3rd ed.). Viking: The Foundation for Inner Peace.

Wood, J. T. (2013). *Interpersonal communication: Everyday encounters* (7th ed.). Melbourne, Australia: Wadsworth, Cengage Learning.

# About the Author

Cillín Hearns is an Irishman loving his life in New Zealand. He is the owner and director of Results Coaching, a leadership coaching company, that focuses on the personal and professional development of IT and business professionals through one-on-one, team and group coaching.

Giving back to the leadership and coaching community is important to Cillín. He founded and facilitates the Wellington Leadership Group which consists of nearly 2,000 members and speaks on a range of topics on everything from holding difficult conversations and giving feedback to personal effectiveness and high-performing teams.

Cillín lives in Wellington with his beautiful wife and his two beautiful daughters.